JOUR
THROUGH
TIME

Also by Soozi Holbeche

The Power of Gems and Crystals
The Power of Your Dreams
Awakening to Change

Journeys Through Time

A Guide to Reincarnation and Your Immortal Soul

Soozi Holbeche

PIATKUS

Acknowledgements

With love and appreciation to all those whose sharing of their own journeys through time led to this book. Especial appreciation to Desmond for his help, and to Paul Solomon, from whom I learned so much.

© 1995 Soozi Holbeche

First published in 1995 by
Judy Piatkus (Publishers) Ltd
5 Windmill Street, London W1P 1HF

The moral right of the author has been asserted

A catalogue record for this book
is available from the British Library

ISBN 0-7499-1466-1

Set in 11½/13½pt Sabon
by Computerset, Harmondsworth

Printed and bound in Great Britain by Bookcraft (Bath) Ltd.

For Desmond Meiring Rice

With all my love.

Same old slippers,
Same old rice,
Same old glimpse
of paradise.

WILLIAM JAMES CAMPTON
(1859–1917)

CONTENTS

It seems to me I have always lived. And I possess memories which go back to the Pharaohs. I see myself very clearly in different professions and in many sorts of fortune. My present personality is the result of my lost personalities. Many things would be explained if we could know our real genealogy. Thus heredity is a just principle which has been badly applied.

GUSTAVE FLAUBERT, Letter to George Sand, 1866

Perhaps I lived before
In some strange world where first my world
  was shaped.
And all this passionate love, and joy, and pain,
That come, I know not whence, and sway my
  deeds,
Are old impetuous memories, blind yet strong,
That this world stirs within me.

GEORGE ELIOT, The Spanish Gypsy

INTRODUCTION

I do not remember a time in my life when I did not believe in reincarnation, and each year that I live reinforces this belief.

In the past this did not help to make my life easy. I remember at school – a strict Catholic convent – asking what the word 'metempsychosis' meant, having discovered it in a book. I now know it is a term sometimes used for reincarnation – *metem* meaning change or growth, and *psyche* meaning soul – implying the evolution of the soul through the process of re-birth. However, from the reaction of the nuns I might have named a sexually-transmitted disease. I was rapped smartly across the knuckles with a ruler, and despatched to the Reverend Mother, who told me I was a heretic and ordered me to stand outside the classroom for the next three days.

On another occasion, a friend of my mother's, Joan, asked me what I was doing. At that time my work was almost exclusively with cancer patients, and when I told her this Joan said: 'Oh, how terrible! I could never do anything like that. I'm far too sensitive.' I explained that my belief in reincarnation and the existence of the soul, whether in or out of the body, enabled me to work with people, no matter what their physical condition. I added that I admired the courage of people all over the world for the way some of them chose to learn, grow and evolve, especially when the lessons came through physical suffering and disability. If I could help someone find the cause of a problem, or help them release from the physical body without fear, my work was worthwhile.

Joan was outraged. 'You don't mean to tell me that souls pop in and out of this or that body at the drop of a hat like a Jack-in-the-Box. It's quite absurd, and as for thinking that a person would choose to live in great poverty or pain – well, that's the most ridiculous thing I've ever heard!' No matter how much I tried to explain my belief that a soul chooses certain situations for the personality to experience in order to develop character and understand the laws of Karma, the laws of cause and effect, she refused to listen and treated me as if I were a lunatic, to the extent that my mother summoned a psychiatrist to the house to see if I was in fact mad. Fortunately for me, he pronounced me sane.

Not long after this episode, I was taken by a friend to have dinner at a very smart London restaurant. As the waiter presented the menu with a flourish, Jim leaned forward and said *sotto voce*: 'She's a vegetarian.' The waiter gasped, fell back, gazed at me and said: 'I'm so *very, very* sorry!' 'Not only that,' said Jim, 'She's a reincarnationist.' This was too much for the waiter. He disappeared to the kitchen and sent someone else to our table. I'm sure he too thought the words 'vegetarian' and 'reincarnation' implied some terrible aberration of nature which was highly infectious.

Today many of the ideas that were considered taboo in the past (even a mere 20 or 30 years ago) are now freely bandied about in normal, everyday newspapers and magazines. Headlines such as 'Reincarnation is making a Comeback', 'Feel your old Self again', or 'Ghostbuster releases Earthbound Souls' raise not a ripple of resistance but rather trigger intense enquiry and conversation. Films and books on past, present and future existence, to say nothing of what happens between lives, are instant sell-outs. Radio and television regularly produce programmes on psychic phenomena, near-death experience, abduction by extra-terrestrial powers. Advertisements such as 'You too can have an out of body experience' or 'Find your Soul Mate' or 'Talk to a Dolphin' are placed and accepted without apology or explanation. A vegetarian diet is now known to prolong life, health and joy.

As a child, I felt reincarnation's timeless quality. I grew up seeing past, present and future simultaneously. It was like looking at chunks of time and events side by side in a spiral – a little like the old-fashioned wire racks for storing gramophone records. A person's face in front of me would suddenly dissolve into another face, of a different race, sex and era. Sometimes six or eight different faces would emerge from the person I looked at – some rising above the head and some merging from left to right.

It was often confusing. I not only saw the past, present and future of the people around me, but also of the trees, houses, bricks and stones. I felt a strong connection to certain animals and a sense of having known them from another time and space. I soon learned to say very little about what I saw, because it always got me into trouble. It was also frequently painful. Suddenly to see the person in front of me dissolve into a Roman warrior or Nazi or SS soldier pricked me with their unresolved energy from the past. It was almost like being pierced with a sword or knife. Often I could barely breathe, and would walk away.

I am sure that some of my beliefs about reincarnation or metempsychosis came from these experiences. Others come from spontaneous recall of other lives that unexpectedly shed light on certain events, relationships, health, fears and other problems, which I had previously been unable to heal or change.

Still others of my beliefs came from past life therapists and researchers with whom I had worked, such as Dr Helen Wambach, Raymond Moody, Paul Solomon, Lynn Buess and William David.

I believe that we choose a certain blueprint for life that gives us the opportunity to grow. To consider the possibility of reincarnation changes our lives, helps us to understand that who we are now is the result of what we were, and that who we shall be in the future depends on what we do now. The spiritual law of Karma, and reincarnation, teach understanding and responsibility, not blind acceptance of fate. They open the idea that we may have been members of other races, religions, and social castes, and shall be again. So how can we despise the differences now? If I hate left-footed Latvians, their food, environment and history, I am quite likely to be born again surrounded by left-footed Latvians, or be one myself.

No matter who or what we were in the past, the only thing that really matters is who we are now, and how we handle the challenges facing us now. Many of these challenges, whether in the form of physical disability, stress in relationships, fears, phobias, addictions, inhibiting attitudes towards ourselves (such as lack of self-esteem) and others, can be faced and overcome by looking at the lives that set them in motion. Even people who do not believe in reincarnation and say 'it's just imagination' have successfully overcome problems in this way.

In my own life a major challenge was my annihilating fear of public speaking. When I began work with Paul

Solomon, spiritual teacher and mystic, who was himself a brilliant and entertaining speaker, he frequently and without warning plucked me from his audience, pushed me onto a stage in front of 800 or 900 people, and muttered out of the side of his mouth 'Speak!' Whereupon he disappeared to the back of the theatre. Paralysed with fright, and blank about what I was meant to say, I usually fell flat on my face as I stepped onto the stage, kicked over the water or the flowers, and dropped the microphone. With a chalk-white face, thumping heart and churning stomach, I opened my mouth to speak, and usually had to do this three or four times before a single word emerged.

Over and over again, due to my overwhelming fear and dread, I made a complete fool of myself. Returning one evening from a particularly disastrous performance, I sank into a chair, closed my eyes and said: 'God, if You expect me to do this work I'll end up in a lunatic asylum!' After a few moments I opened my eyes and had the strangest sense of being in a male body, wearing a toga and holding a stone tablet under my left arm. I appeared to be delivering a message to a group of men and women who wore brilliantly coloured silk robes. My message was simple: 'Look at what you are doing with your lives, and love one another!'

The people laughed and began to mock me. I became irritated and stamped my foot. 'Love one another!' I cried with greater force, which quickly turned to anger. Just as quickly, the crowd's mood also erupted into anger, and they stoned me to death. I felt the pain of stones hitting my throat, and not being able to breathe. (I have also had, in this life, fears of choking to death.) In that moment, an incredible rage rose within me. Rage with God, who sent me to do this task, and yet must have known the outcome. Rage and despair with myself that my message of love had aroused so much hate that I was stoned to death. (I also realised that one of my lessons from that life was that you can't teach love with will.) I also felt anger and a sense of betrayal towards the people who killed me.

As I came out of the experience I saw, as if at the movies, a sequence of images of myself in different lives, both as a male and female, doing similar work which always appeared to end in my death. I saw myself tortured, beheaded, imprisoned, sacrificed, disembowelled, burnt, poisoned, and even walled up and left to die. (Obviously, I never delivered the message correctly.)

I suddenly realised that every time I stood in front of a group of people to speak – 'to deliver the message' – the soul memory of 'this is going to be the death of me' was so strong that my body went into an imitation of the death pangs. My bladder gave way, my heart and circulation went haywire, I could not breathe or speak. Incredible emotional energy was released through this completely spontaneous remembering. It was painful, powerful, and life-changing. I was 85 per cent healed of my fear of public speaking. I can still feel stirrings of discomfort today, especially in front of a large group, but I just hug myself and say: 'It's okay', as if I were reassuring a vulnerable child.

Since then I have remembered many other lives, usually spontaneously, sometimes through dreams, and occasionally with trusted past-life therapists. Each life remembered has contributed insight and understanding of why I am the way I am today and, because these memories have also helped me to expand my vision of the universe and my place in it, they have both empowered me, and improved the quality of my life.

During the past twenty-five years as a counsellor/healer/therapist, I have travelled and worked with hundreds of people of different colours, creeds and races. Some of this book is about them, their own past-life experiences and the effect on their lives today. Some of it is in response to the many questions I am asked about reincarnation, Karma, birth, death and dying, soul and life purpose, past life or regression therapy, what happens between lives, relationships, group incarnations, soul mates and families. I can only share from my own experiences and those of my patients, and do not claim to be an authority on all these subjects.

At the end of this book you will find many different exercises and suggestions as to how to discover aspects of yourself that may stem from this or other lives. All of them are simple, easy to follow, and bring results. Some may be more effective than others. The only way to find out what works best for you is to try. And when you try, do not compare your experience with someone else's. Don't think that your next-door neighbour is more spiritually evolved because he or she can recall past lives at will, and you find it difficult. Like learning to drive a car, it is simply a matter of practice.

For many people the idea of reincarnation is a fantasy. For others it makes absolute sense to think of the earth plane as a school, offering a billion choices of experiences ranging from kindergarten to university and masters' degrees. To consider the possibility of other lives, other selves (maybe co-existing with us in simultaneous realities, as I saw in childhood), can change each moment, each meeting, each event, each relationship, and imbue it with importance.

To quote Henry Ford:

I adopted the theory of reincarnation when I was twenty-six ... Religion offered nothing to the point ... Even work could not give me complete satisfaction. Work is futile if we cannot utilize the experience we collect in one world in the next. When

I discovered reincarnation it was as if I had found a universal plan. I realized that there was a chance to work out my ideas. Time was no longer limited. I was no longer a slave to the hands of the clock . . . Genius is experience. Some seem to think that it is a gift or talent, but it is the fruit of long experience in many lives. Some are older souls than others, so they know more . . .

The discovery of reincarnation put my mind at ease . . . If you preserve a record of this conversation write it so that it puts men's minds at ease. I would like to communicate to others the calmness that the long view of life gives us.

1

REINCARNATION

In contrast to Reincarnation and Karma all other views appear petty and narrow ... Only the profoundly conceived idea of Reincarnation could give me any consolation, since that belief shows how all at last can reach complete redemption.

RICHARD WAGNER

Reincarnation has been either accepted, dreamed of, imagined, desired, discussed, mocked, or reviled by billions of people, probably since the world began.

Reincarnation, as part of the law of Karma, opens up to us the idea that we experience this life either happily or with suffering according to our actions and attitudes in other lives. To Western minds, this can seem fearful or punitive. In the East, it leads to an understanding that 'this action will produce this result'. Therefore, by conscious acceptance of a kind of cosmic accountancy across many centuries, we bring harmony into our lives.

In the schools of Ancient Wisdom (sometimes called the Mystery Schools) of China, Tibet, Greece and Egypt, the concept of Reincarnation and the Law of Karma were an automatic part of the curriculum. Students preparing for initiation into the mysteries were shown that nothing happened by accident, that every event, day or night, and their response to it, no matter how small or how big, was part of the training which would ultimately lead to their soul's evolution.

Re-birth And Duality

The theory of Reincarnation presupposes that the soul and spirit of man is immortal, and must journey towards wisdom and enlightenment through myriad experiences on many different planes – planes representing different levels of consciousness. This theory also implies that we who live on earth are enrolled in one of the most powerful 'Schools of the Mysteries' of all time. We are offered billions of different types and grades of lessons, opportunities and challenges.

Each of us is all the sums he has not counted, subtract us into nakedness and night again and you shall see begin in Crete four thousand years ago the love that ended yesterday in Texas. Each moment is the fruit of 4,000 years.

THOMAS WOLFE, *Look Homeward Angel*

To develop spiritual understanding requires many lifetimes, both as male and female. These lifetimes must include every facet of human event and emotion; doubt, fear, hate, rejection, sorrow, loss, despair, jealousy and punishment, as well as love, joy, power, success and happiness. If we only knew love, we would never understand someone else who felt unloved and desperate lashing out and causing deliberate damage. If we only knew freedom, we would never understand the feelings of a prisoner behind bars for thirty years. To live on the earth is to live on a planet of duality, where we learn to value the positive through experiencing the negative. For example, if I have starved in this or another life, I shall value food and not waste it. If, as a soldier, I have killed, maimed or tortured my enemy, or been tortured by him, I am going to value peace. Eventually we learn that one experience leads to joy, another to pain and confusion. We learn to respect the law of cause and effect, of Karma. If I do, or do not do, this or that, this is the result. Karma teaches us that we only truly learn by experience, and not from a guru or by studying a philosophical book.

It is similar to a child playing with matches. His mother sees him and, snatching the matches from him, says: 'You must not do this. You'll burn yourself or set the house alight, or start a forest fire.' As soon as she is out of sight he relights the matches and, sure enough, his fingers and clothes are burnt and the house is in flames. It is only now that he really understands what his mother was talking about.

Like the child, who now realises from his own involvement, that flame from a match can cause warmth and comfort or pain and destruction, we too, as we progress, develop the wisdom to discriminate between the old, new or repeated experiences.

The idea of Reincarnation or re-birth offers the opportunity for change and progress, but says it is up to us to make use of these opportunities. We can choose whether to unfold into the light, or to remain ignorant in the dark.

The soul passes from form to form, and the mansions of her pilgrimage are manifold. Thou puttest off thy bodies as raiment, and as vesture thou doest fold them up. Thou art from old, O soul of man, yea thou art from everlasting.

HERMES TRISMEGISTUS, *Egyptian Hermetic Fragments*

Past civilisations accepted re-birth as naturally as they

accepted the ebb and flow of the sea, the appearance and disappearance of the sun and the moon, the cycles of spring, summer, autumn and winter. Through nature, they aligned to the rhythm of birth, death, and re-birth in a way that we, in a world of technology, science and mechanisation, have separated ourselves from. For too long, we have celebrated the power of the intellect at the expense of the spirit.

Ancient peoples lived in a rhythm of understanding that is well described in the following words from the Bible:

> *To everything there is a season*
> *And a time to every purpose under the heaven,*
> *A time to be born and a time to die,*
> *A time to plant and a time to pluck up*
> *That which is planted,*
> *A time to kill and a time to heal,*
> *A time to break down and a time to build up.*
> *A time to weep, and a time to laugh,*
> *A time to mourn and a time to dance,*
> *A time to cast away stones, and a time*
> *To gather stones together,*
> *A time to get and a time to lose,*
> *A time to keep and a time to cast away,*
> *A time to rend and a time to sew,*
> *A time to keep silence and a time to speak.*
> *A time to love and a time to hate,*
> *A time of war and a time of peace.*
>
> *Eccles. 3:1–8*

Maybe these words also suggest the idea of infinite cycles of many lives. Edgar Cayce, described as America's greatest mystic, whose powers of clairvoyance led to miraculous insight into the realms of before, now and after life, once said: 'The plan for the soul was a cycle of experience unlimited in scope and direction, in which the new individual would come to know creation in all its aspects, at the discretion of will. The cycle would be completed when the desire of the will was no longer different from the Will of God.' In other words, the soul purpose for each incarnation is reunion and re-identification with the Source of Life. The life purpose is how we go about it.

Knowledge of the Mysteries – the deepest beliefs of man's origin, physical nature, and connection to divine and supernatural worlds – has been discovered in the sacred texts and philosophical understanding of hundreds of different religions and civilisations. Egyptians, Buddhists, Hindus, Chinese Taoists, Jews, Eskimos, Greeks, Romans, Africans, Australian Aboriginals, American Indians, Theosophists, Sufis, Zoroastrians, Rosicrucians, Freemasons, and many, many more have a history of belief in reincarnation, Karma (some also in transmigration, sometimes thought of as transference into an animal body – usually because of 'bad' behaviour) and the evolution of the soul. They were taught that man's liberation came through knowledge, and that the doctrine of Metempsychosis, of many lives, was an intrinsic part of that knowledge.

Reincarnation And Established Religion

Many Westeners associate reincarnationist beliefs with Eastern or Oriental religions. The Vedas, Upanishads (considered to be part of the esoteric or inner teaching of the Vedas), Tibetan Book of the Dead, and Bhagavad Gita are permeated with the idea of the passage of the soul from body to body. However, some of our best-known thinkers, from Pythagoras, Socrates, Plato, Apollonius and Plotinus to Victor Hugo, William James, D. H. Lawrence, Bertrand Russell, Carl Jung and hundreds of others also freely accepted the philosophy of 'I am here, and shall return again.'

The Jewish Cabbala, representing the hidden wisdom of the Old Testament, says that reincarnation is an essential part of its doctrine. In the 17th century, Rabbi Manesseh, a theologian and statesman, wrote: 'The belief or the doctrine of the transmigration of souls is a firm and infallible dogma accepted by the whole assemblage of our church with one accord, so there is none to be found who would dare to deny it . . . Indeed, there are a great number of sages in Israel who hold firm to this doctrine, so that they made it a dogma, a fundamental part of our religion.' A quote from the Cabbala mentioned in the *Talmudic Miscellany* says: 'If a man be niggardly either in a financial or a spiritual regard, giving nothing of his money to the poor, or not implanting of his knowledge to the ignorant, he shall be punished by transmigration into a woman.'

Early Christian theologians, priests, and Church Fathers thought, and even taught, that pre-existence of the soul and future re-birth was a truth beyond question. The soul 'exchanges one man for another man, so that the life of humanity is continued always by means of the same soul,' wrote Saint Gregory of Nazianzus, a 4th-century Bishop of Constantinople. One of the best-known exponents of this philosophy was Origen, a Greek once described by Saint Jerome as 'the greatest teacher of the Church after the Apostles'. However, he like many other theologians, later declared that Origen's writings and beliefs on immortality were heresies. In AD553, at the Second Council of Constantinople presided over by the Emperor Justinian, it was decided that Origen and his teachings were anathema – or cursed to damnation. So too were his followers, and anyone else who preached the doctrine of Metempsychosis.

The branding of the concept of pre-existence as anathema led the Council to reject almost all passages in the Bible that referred to reincarnation. It also brought about several centuries of persecution, torture and death for tens of thousands of people in the so-called 'Holy War' of the Inquisition.

Groups across Western Europe such as the Cathars (the word comes from cartharsis or purification), Albigenses (a branch of Catharism), Rosicrucians, Knights Templar and Troubadours kept the philosophy of re-birth quietly alive in secret documents, by word of mouth, and through plays, poems and songs. Many of the Grail stories are believed to be the means by which the scriptures of the Albigenses were both preserved and presented, usually by travelling Troubadours.

The Gnosticism (the term comes from the Greek word *gnosis*, knowledge) of the Cathars aroused the ire of the Church to fever point. The Albigenses were destroyed, and soldiers and clergy murdered hundreds of other men, women and children too. The siege of Montségur is one of the better known of these massacres, partly through the books of Arthur Guirdham, a medical doctor a few of whose patients began to show symptoms of severe depression, burning and torture around the anniversary of the slaughter of Montségur. Later, through dreams, spontaneous recall and regression, they remembered their earlier names, and all the relevant details of this agonising event. These details were later verified, and resulted in Dr Guirdham's books, some of which are *The Cathars and Reincarnation*, *The Lake and the Castle*, and *We are One Another*.

Dr Guirdham believed that these memories, which included his own Cathar background, surfaced because of the urgent need to make clear the importance of reincarnation. In 1978 during a talk entitled 'Evidence for Group Incarnation' I heard him say: 'The world is drowning in materialism. It is therefore necessary to pass on, to those disposed to hear, the truth about the existence of an immaterial, important component, the psyche, which learns on earth and between lives those lessons which enable us ultimately to fuse with the individualised spirit and, through it, with the ultimate source of being.'

The fanatical opposition by the Church to so-called heretics, such as the Cathars, drove reincarnation underground until fairly recently – although, of course, every century has had wise men, scholars, writers and philosophers who have quietly upheld beliefs about the soul's passage through many lifetimes.

As Christianity was introduced to the world by a teacher of righteousness, love, compassion, peace and forgiveness, the fact that professed Christians could kill, and condemn to eternal damnation other Christians holding different opinions on some issues, is quite extraordinary.

I experienced a little of this contradiction when I first went to South Africa about 16 years ago. A church synod composed of Dutch Reform ministers invited me to a meeting at which I was to answer questions. I happily agreed, and turned up to find myself on a platform facing a large number of dark-suited men. The first question put to me was: 'Do you think anyone like Jesus Christ has ever walked this earth, either before or since his life and crucifixion?' I thought about it and finally said: 'Yes and no. I think Jesus was a highly evolved and extraordinary man. I do not think he was Jesus Christ at the beginning, but became "Christed" during the last three years of his ministry – in other words, overshadowed by the Christ consciousness which I see as a kind of very powerful ray of energy emanating from God. I believe every nation and civilisation has had, at least once in the course of its history, similar messengers and teachers who were also empowered by the Christ energy or Divine inspiration.' I named Buddha, Zoroaster, Mohammed, Lao Tzu, amongst those who have helped anchor Divine or Metaphysical energy in the earth through their lives and teachings. A voice from the audience said: 'I suppose you believe in reincarnation too?' 'Yes,' I replied. Whereupon these ministers rose to their feet in uproar and said: 'You are blasphemous, evil! You are of the devil!' I felt as if I faced the Inquisition, and was glad to be hustled out.

A vast transformation will take place in life when the ideas of reincarnation and Karma are no longer held by a few people . . . The whole configuration of the planet, as well as the social life of men in their future, depends upon how men have lived in earlier incarnations . . .

RUDOLF STEINER

The problem with many orthodox Christian religions is the teaching that Jesus was a martyr who died to save us from our sins, which annuls the ancient Karmic law of cause and effect. This is because these Christian religions insist that our salvation comes through confession, repentance, the intercession of priests and clergy, and even, in the past, by payment for 'indulgences'. If you could not or would not pay, then no salvation. This, combined with the terror aroused by hundreds of years of Inquisition, gave the Church inordinate power and influence which often, instead of inspiring joy and happiness, was misused to instil fear, guilt, a sense of worthlessness, and dependency, in the hearts and minds of many devout Christians. They also decreed that life was a one-time opportunity, which led to heaven, hell, or purgatory.

Reincarnation and Karma imply personal responsibility (maybe this is why many people find the idea frightening), self-reliance and individual empowerment. 'No matter what my situation is at the moment, I put myself there, and can get myself out of it.' I am not a victim. Reincarnation optimistically says that we have much time and many chances to get it right as we journey back to God. We can still pray for help, forgiveness and understanding, but we must take action ourselves. It is a bit like going on diet or overcoming an addiction to smoking: no one else can do it for us.

In *A Man Seen Afar* Wellesley Tudor Pole, founder of the Chalice Well Trust in Glastonbury and author of many books, is quoted as saying, in a message passed back through a medium after his death, that 'Christians are sometimes horrified that after death they find their own Karmic slates not clean. Purgatory for them consists in the state of shock and disillusionment into which they sink on finding that they alone are responsible for taking the essential steps through which salvation can ultimately be attained.'

Reincarnation And The Modern World

Today research suggests that two-thirds of the world's population believes in past, present and future lives. Much of this interest was kindled in 1875 by the founder of the Theosophical Society, Madame Helene Blavatsky, and her books such as *Isis Unveiled* and *The Secret Doctrine*. The work of Annie Besant, Alice Bailey and Rudolf Steiner stimulated further interest, not only in reincarnation but also in other aspects of spiritual development.

Edgar Cayce, known as the Sleeping Prophet, saw while in a trance how past, present and future wove together to influence the personality, health and life pattern of each person who came to him for a reading. Initially shocked at the idea of reincarnation, and imagining that the devil was in his subconscious, he was forced to change his mind when the accuracy of his readings and predictions was verified. Cayce's work turned upside down the conventional idea of heredity. Once, when someone asked, 'From which side of my family do I inherit most?' Cayce replied: 'You have inherited most from yourself, not from your family. The family is only a river through which the soul flows.' Despite his original disbelief in reincarnation, he predicted his own return to earth in 1998.

Deservedly, Edgar Cayce's work is now known internationally. In 1931 The Association of Research and Enlightenment (A.R.E.) was formed, to both study and disseminate Cayce's readings worldwide.

A fascinating case for reincarnation is the way in which a 'new' Dalai Lama is chosen. Each Dalai Lama is believed to be a reincarnation of the previous one. The search, which involves prayer, consultation of a monk oracle, psychic visions, symbols, dreams, and other indications, eventually leads to a child who must identify objects belonging to the previous god-King. The current 14th Dalai Lama, at two years old, correctly identified rosaries and a walking stick and drum belonging to his predecessor, as well as the names of his fellow Lamas, before being pronounced the returned Dalai Lama.

Dorothy Eady, who claimed to be the reincarnation of Bentreshyt, the priestess lover of King Seti I in Ancient Egypt, lived out her beliefs to the extent that not only did other people see Seti appear, but she also ended her life caring for the Temple of Seti, and telling stories of Egyptian lives that inspired hundreds of others.

Later books by Joan Grant, Arthur Ford, Ruth Montgomery, Lobsang Rampa, all describing undying worlds of before, between and after, burst upon the world, to be followed in the 1950s by the Bridie Murphy story about an American housewife who under hypnosis claimed to remember a life in 18th-century Ireland. This story, described in the book *The Search for Bridie Murphy*, created enormous controversy as to its truth. It also caused an explosion of interest in the phenomenon of reincarnation and past-life recall. In the 1970s the Bloxham tapes (recorded interviews made by a doctor with his patients about their past lives) were shown on BBC television, and also created a sensation – especially the one in which a Welsh housewife remembered a life as a Jewish woman, Rebecca, living in York in the 12th century, and hounded to death during uprisings against the Jews in 1189.

I have been forced to consider the possibility of reincarnation, which in the past I had thought a ridiculous belief.

CARL ROGERS

Gradually researchers, psychologists, doctors, psychiatrists, and therapists brought what was previously considered forbidden, irrational, or just plain fantasy, into the mainstream of current thinking. Denys Kelsey (husband of Joan Grant), Helen Wambach, Edith Fiore, Morris Netherton, Raymond Moody and Elizabeth Kübler-Ross (famous for her work on death and dying), all of them well-known doctors and psychiatrists, began to use past-life therapy as normally as they might take a pulse or a temperature. Many of their patients suffering a variety of fears, phobias, allergies, addictions, compulsions, and ordinary physical symptoms recovered, often

instantly, on recalling the life in which the problem originated. (I shall describe case histories to illustrate this in
later chapters.)

Dr Ian Stevenson is probably one of the best-known of
all reincarnation researchers, having investigated
hundreds of cases, most of which concern children.
According to Dr Stevenson, who is renowned for his
painstaking and scientific methods of investigation, we
are on the brink of proving reincarnation to be an
irrefutable truth. He also says that many of us suffer from
a fear of new ideas, which causes instant rejection of
anything that does not fit our current concept of reality,
or for which there appears to be no concrete evidence.

As I said in my book *Awakening to Change*, when
reincarnation is accepted as a fact of life rather than a
whimsical theory of New Age mystics, people will surely
stop polluting the planet. They will help to create a better
world, knowing that they will return to it.

In the words of Voltaire: 'It is no more surprising to be
born twice than it is to be born once.'

2

KARMA

Whatsoever a man soweth, that shall he also reap.

SAINT PAUL, Epistle to the Galatians, 6:7

It was winter and one o'clock in the morning. I was sixteen years old and stranded at Paddington Station, having missed the last train. Home was five or six hours away, and the next train was not due until dawn. Initially brave, I decided to sit on a bench and wait. However, the dark of night seemed to pulse and throb in a sinister, almost evil way, and prickles of apprehension began to run up and down my spine. A few drunks, bickering over whose turn it was for the next slurp from the last bottle, sprawled under the arches. Stray ghostly figures drifted in and out of the darkness. Bleary-eyed men approached, whispering indecent proposals. Shifting shadows, faint scuffles and cries, the continuous ring of an unanswered phone from a public box, and the muttered curses of an old bagwoman as she settled herself on a pile of rags – all created an atmosphere which for me was pregnant with menace.

In panic, I suddenly remembered that friends of my cousins lived nearby, and I ran out of the station to find them. Ten minutes later, without even a phone call to warn them, I rang the front door bell. After some delay, the door was opened by a man naked to the waist and wearing a towel round his middle. I had never seen him before, but as we stared at each other we both simultaneously gasped: 'It's you!' I felt as if I were falling through time and space, while faintly, in a very dim and distant part of my mind – almost like an echo – I heard a voice say: 'This is your Karma! As the result of what you have done you will see each other only once again.' In that instant, I saw that this was the 'once again'. I also recognised that I knew this man as well as if he were an arm or a leg belonging to my own body. Triggered by his present bare-torsoed, towel-clad appearance, I saw an image from the past in which he was Roman or Greek, wearing a toga. He was a man of authority and power, which we had in some way misused.

Seconds later, back to the present, both of us shocked and confused, I explained not what I had seen and heard in my head, but how I had missed my train and needed to stay the night. This man – I do not even know his name – was on holiday from Portuguese East Africa, and had only just arrived as a guest in the house himself. I slept on the sofa, left early for the station, and never saw him again.

So great an impact had this incident on me that I was led to question and study the meaning and purpose of Karma thoroughly.

I discovered a translation of the *Tibetan Book of the Dead (Bardel Thodol)* and another, smaller book that gave an overall interpretation. The following words leapt out at me from the latter: 'Behind you is the terrifying raging fire of Karma, driving you onward. The full force of Karma engulfs you now ... There are frightening sounds. It is all so terrifying you feel you must flee ...' and further on: 'You are afraid to enter a womb because it may mean a lifetime of suffering with a more imperfect body than the one you had before. This is evidence that evil spirits are influencing you ...'

For days and nights I lived in terror that the numerous deities and evil spirits described in the books would descend from the skies or rise out of the ground and swallow me up. I also thought that maybe the nuns had been right when they told me I was of the devil. I speedily learned to pray:

> *When Karma comes and I am defenceless*
> *May the compassionate one protect me.*
> *When I am tempted into bad Karma*
> *May the Primary clear light come to me.*
> *Om-Mani-Padme-Hum.*

Seeking The Meaning Of Karma

Of course the *Tibetan Book of the Dead* is not meant to inspire fear. It teaches acceptance of what is an inevitable part of life, and that our final moments can be a time of insight, enlightenment and liberation. It explains the different Bardos (stages) through which the soul journeys between lives, and says that after death our actions, habits, attitudes, fears and desires will all have to be faced. However, if at the moment of death we can call or focus upon the Buddha, or anyone else who for us repre-sents the Divine Light of God, we can free ourselves from the need to reincarnate on the physical plane. It says too that Karma not only sets in motion the physical, mental, emotional, and geographical conditions for re-birth, but also provides limitless opportunity for change. At sixteen, however, I believed that death, Karma and re-birth implied punishment for 'bad' thoughts, words and deeds, administered by wrathful deities who assisted God in counting them up.

I scoured bookshops, libraries, and even newsagents for

any publication that mentioned the magic word 'Karma'. I avidly read books by an eclectic variety of authors ranging from Eastern mystics, Tibetan lamas and Indian gurus to Cabbalists, Theosophists, psychics, mediums and occultists. While one or two interpreted Karma as Divine retribution, most spoke of Reincarnation and Karma as principle and fundamental Laws of the Universe, a divine system of balance, counter-balance, and perfect justice; a system in which nothing happens by accident.

My brothers, each man's life the outcome of his former living is; the bygone wrongs bring forth sorrows and woes. The bygone right breeds bliss . . . this is the doctrine of Karma.

BUDDHA

No child is born deaf, blind or dumb, no man or woman is rich or poor, savage or civilised, powerful or powerless, without purpose, planning and influence from the past. No birth is a random event, but a carefully orchestrated means of accomplishing certain tasks that will ultimately serve the soul on its journey back to its source.

I saw that Karma is not only the Law of Cause and Effect, but also the working out of that Law. Instead of chastisement *for* our sins and omissions, Karma implies correction *by* them. In being on the receiving end of what we ourselves have at some time done, we face ourselves rather than a castigating judge. This life is the mirror reflection of many others. Just as a mirror helps us to adjust or change our physical appearance, so can the mirror of Karma help us spiritually to adjust and change. In the words of Padmasambhana, a Tibetan saint: 'If you want to know your past life, look into your present condition; if you want to know your future life, look at your present actions.'

Karma is also sometimes called the Law of Attraction, by which like attracts like. Another way of saying this is that Karma is created by our attachment to our deeds and misdeeds, or those of others, rather than by the deeds themselves. This attachment can come through lack of forgiveness, or through resentment, fear, anger, revenge, guilt (to name but a few), and even from a belief in the need for punishment. 'I am an unworthy sinner, and must suffer the consequences.'

My own present life has many examples of the consequences of attachment to painful memories from the past – although I was not initially aware of these memories. In one life, in front of my then daughter, I was raped and disembowelled by soldiers. I died cursing them, which created this-life Karma I had to work through in the following way: due to complications from German measles, I had a Caesarian termination of a five-month pregnancy, which could be described as the modern equivalent of my past disembowelment. I developed an unrealistic dislike of the doctor who performed the operation, as well as for the long jagged scar on my stomach. Rationally, I knew that the doctor had done his best to help me. Irrationally, I could not bear to be in his presence. (Excessive dislike, hate, revulsion, all indicate a Karmic bond to be worked out, just as instant rapport, love and liking suggest 'good' Karma, to be enjoyed and accepted.) My scar was a constant source of hatred and suffering, so much so that I eventually asked myself 'why?' Immediately the past-life memory popped up, and I saw that the doctor had been the soldier who seized the first sword to open my belly, long ago. Today he used his sword, or knife, to heal. I was finally able to accept, forgive and release what had happened. However, in order to do this I had to re-experience something of it.

In another life, during the French revolution, I was

guillotined. Because the first attempt to knock off my head failed – the descending blade hit my jaw and not my neck – I was guillotined twice. Apparently I again died cursing, hating and full of revenge, which also dramatically affected my present life. I smashed my face in an accident, dislocated my jaw three times, and developed osteo-arthritis in my mandibular joints. The combination of these experiences, together with the re-surfacing of the memory of what set them in motion, led to a complete healing: the energy locked into my jaw was released.

I cannot think of permanent emnity between man and man, and, believing as I do in the theory of re-birth, I live in the hope that, if not in this birth, in some other birth I shall be able to hug all humanity in a friendly embrace.

MAHATMA GANDHI

My refusal to surrender – to forgive and forget at the moment of death, in both cases – drew me, 'like attracts like', to similar situations in the present, until I cleared them. Much of our Karma sorts itself out without need to remember the cause, but if we do remember, through past-life therapy, dreams, or spontaneous recall, it gives us greater understanding of the 'why' of certain events in our lives. The main point to remember is that to re-live the past is to re-lieve the present and so re-create the future.

Karma is not only personal and individual, but intimately connected to family, race, village or city, country, society and religion. We also deal with planetary Karma through the particular evolutionary cycle or century in which we incarnate.

According to Edgar Cayce, many previous inhabitants of the legendary sunken continent of Atlantis are now back, mainly living in America. Atlantis was finally destroyed through greed, corruption, competition, and selfishness. Reincarnated Atlantean/Americans now have the opportunity to put right what they previously did wrong. Dreamwork, meditation and journal-writing have taught me that if I have a question I will get an answer. So I asked if President Nixon had an Atlantean incarnation. I was told: 'Yes, he was a Prince of Atlantis, but misused his power. This present life is his opportunity to use power correctly.' (At the same time I questioned the pre-existent identities of the Kennedys, and was told: 'The Borgias.' Believe it or not, the answers did seem to fit!) Edgar Cayce also said about national Karma that: 'Every nation will finally suffer its bad deeds.' To illustrate this, he described how the Spanish Conquistadores had come back as victims of the Spanish Inquisition.

The Cabbala puts it like this: 'Our free will, leading to wilful, will-less, or willing actions, generates what in India is called Karma, and in Cabbala reward and punishment to the third and fourth generations.' So each act directed against the world and its people has an equal and reverberating reaction on ourselves, either immediately or in the future.

Resolution Of Pain

In the course of my work many people have come to me for regression therapy, and in the process recalled lives in Germany in World War II, some as victims of persecution, some as persecutors. In delving into these lives, it appears that this war helped to clear an enormous weight of negativity that hung over the planet like a pall from centuries of torture during the Inquisition. Many of the 'victims' went even further back into memories: for example, of lives in Rome, where they threw Christians to the lions, or galloping through the Russian Steppes with Genghis Khan on missions of pillage and plunder. Most of the 'persecutors' are now working as doctors, dentists, osteopaths, chiropractors, nurses and psychologists.

Two exceptions to this were Carol and Lorraine, both of whom I met long after my interest in Karma began. Carol was 21 when she broke her neck in a diving accident. Paralysed from her neck to her toes, Carol found it hard to adjust to life in a wheelchair. Two years later she lost her left leg in a car accident in which her sister died.

Later, through past-life therapy, Carol saw she had been a brilliant surgeon/scientist in World War II's German concentration camps. Obsessed with Nazism and her scientific skills, Carol mercilessly performed organ transplants, amputations and genetic experiments on thousands of men, women and children. Carol realised that she was now suffering many of the physical indignities she had inflicted on her helpless victims. She also felt that many of her own doctors expressed the same clinical detachment towards her today as she had shown to her patients of the past.

This knowledge – with her understanding that she had *voluntarily* taken on her present-life sufferings, despite their severity ('to get it all over in one go') imbued Carol with the courage to fight back, to get as much as she could out of life despite her limitations. She now works for a firm of architects to ensure that their building plans include adequate provision for wheelchairs and disabled people.

Like Carol, Lorraine suddenly tapped into a life in Nazi Germany. Not only that but, as if she were telling me the story of a dream, Lorraine began to describe the atrocities committed by Ilsa Koch, who became known as the Witch of Buchenwald. Ilsa, among other crimes against humanity, made lampshades out of human skin and pulled out teeth and finger and toenails with no anaesthetic, simply to observe her victims' reactions to pain.

Lorraine's initial thought that she herself was the reincarnation of Ilsa Koch changed to the realisation that she had been Ilsa's assistant. Lorraine then saw that Lou, her two-year-old daughter, was in fact the born-again Ilsa, and that their Karma together was to accept, and then work through, what they had done in the past. (Lorraine and I spent 30 days together in order to process this life. When I met Lou for the first time she was the living image of a Nazi concentration-camp victim – a hollow-eyed, sunken-cheeked shadow of what a normal healthy child looks like. Today, some 15 years later, both Lorraine and Lou appear to be leading happy lives.)

Karmically, we swing between being the murderer and the murdered, the prostitute and the nun, the poor ragged builder of the Great Wall of China and the king in his castle. In fact, in one session a woman saw herself murdered three times – but added: 'I get extra points every time I'm murdered.' In the *Bhagavad Gita*, Krishna says to Arjuna:

> *He who in his ignorance thinketh: 'I slay', or 'I am slain', babbleth like an infant lacking knowledge. Of a truth, none can slay, none can be slain. Verily, the Real Man – the Spirit of Man – is neither born, nor doth it die. Unborn, undying, ancient, perpetual and eternal, it hath endured, and will endure for ever. The body may die, be slain, be destroyed completely – but he that hath occupied it remaineth unharmed.*

In another session, a man remembered lives as both a nun and a prostitute. He realised that he had developed a hundred times more spiritual awareness as the prostitute than as the nun. If Saint Jerome had known this, maybe would have thought twice before saying, as he did, when he denounced Origen as a heretic in AD402: 'We may have to fear that we, who are now men, may afterwards be born women, and one who is now a virgin may chance to be a prostitute.'

Karma Brings Balance

Karma provides us with myriad opportunities to touch, taste, feel, think, hear and experience every aspect of incarnation into a physical body, in a hundred different guises. Over and over again, we play hero, villain, and everything in between. Gradually, our personalities are honed. We shed, like old clothes that do not fit any more, negative bits and pieces of ourselves, and move into new forms and new experiences.

No matter how bad we are, or have been, there is always hope. Our good is never lost or wiped out. Even the Tibetan saint and poet, Milarepa, initially trained to be a sorcerer, killed, maimed and ruined many people with black magic. Later, however, filled with remorse, and with the help of a teacher who set him difficult tasks and made him undergo severe physical ordeals, Milarepa purified his previous actions. He became enlightened and went on to inspire millions of other people. It is never too late for any of us. As they say in Tibet: 'Negative energy has one good quality: it can be purified.'

Another aspect of Karma is that in any one lifetime we never take on board what is beyond our own individual capacity – although we may certainly feel that 'this is just too much' when disaster strikes. Many other-life actions or inactions boomerang back to us in the form of chronic physical deformity, disability or illness. A blind Australian friend discovered a life in which he pierced out his then enemy's eyes with a spear. Another, now suffering from chronic diabetes, discovered a life similar to that of Caligula who, to put it mildly, over-indulged in the 'sweets' of life. My friend's then licentiousness, cruelty and physical abuse have brought him back now into a sick female body that requires constant attention.

Kathleen, with a club foot, turned back the pages to see that she had had a number of lives as a brilliant dancer. However, her pride in her prowess isolated her from the people around her, and she used her sarcastic wit to mock them. In this life, especially as a young girl at school, she had had to suffer the mockery of others. (We must remember that we create these situations for ourselves, and not at the dictate of an avenging God.)

Of course each illness has its own unique this- or other-life cause, and what I am saying is not intended to imply that all diabetes is the result of abuse, all blindness the result of blinding another. Sometimes we incarnate into a physically disabled body simply to experience its limitation, or as part of a training to be a future healer, or to teach. Great souls often embody enormous handicaps to teach the power of spirit over matter. Helen Keller was an example of this.

Many of my sessions have uncovered illness and accident as a means to inspire, spiritually wake up, or emotionally initiate the family and friends of the person who suffers the problem. For example, a baby born to one family had so many physical defects that he only lived for three weeks. During those three weeks he opened the hearts, not only of his parents, but also all of those involved in his short life. He was a master teacher of unconditional love, and his three weeks on earth left an indelible imprint. It is usually far more painful and life-changing for us to see our children or family suffer than it is to suffer ourselves. Illness can also be a way of learning patience, or to listen or to receive love. Our physical bodies, like our human relationships, are carefully designed to maximise any Karma we need to meet.

No matter what problems and tragedies come into our lives, we can turn them into great good if we will look at them as opportunities to grow. Elizabeth Kübler-Ross says: 'If you experience losses you can take the pain and learn to accept it, not as a curse or a punishment, but as a gift to you, a gift with a very specific purpose.' That exactly describes a Karmic event – a gift with a very specific purpose.

Creating Good Karma

Karma in Sanskrit means action, or the law of continuity in action, which means the flow of energy between events (positive and negative) and their outcomes. Karma means that we are interconnected, interrelated, to the whole of life. Nothing happens in isolation. Every single thing we do, say, think or feel, no matter how small, big, good, bad or indifferent, produces a result and affects everything and everyone else on the planet. It is said that even the flutter of a butterfly's wings will cause a response in the rainforests of South America. By the same token, my spray-deodorant or insect-repellent contributes to the destruction of the ozone layer.

A woman describing her NDE (near-death experience) said: 'Everything went by for review. I was ashamed of a lot of things I'd done, not only for myself, but how I affected other people. I found that not even our thoughts are lost.' She went on to describe the effects of our thoughts, words and deeds, not only on each other, but also on the weather, plants, animals and the landscape. The first step therefore in creating good Karma is to take responsibility for our thoughts.

The concept of re-birth necessarily implies the continuity of personality. Here the human personality is
regarded as continuous and accessible to memory, so
that when one is incarnated or born one is able, at
least potentially, to remember that one has lived
through previous existences, and that these
existences were one's own, i.e. that they had the same
ego-form as the present life. As a rule, reincarnation
means re-birth in a human body.

C. J. JUNG from a 1939 lecture,
'Concerning Re-Birth'

Some religions believe that if you have very bad Karma
you will be re-born as an animal or an insect. I personally
believe, though I may be wrong, that human and animal
consciousness are of two different streams. I believe that
animals do evolve and reincarnate as we do, but maybe
animal Karma is to move from being a wild, man-eating
tiger to being eaten by man as a sheep or a cow, and from
there to become man's companion in the form of a cat or
a dog or a horse, then perhaps to evolve in intelligence
and become an animal-actor or a circus performer. (I
mean having the intelligence to do this – not because I
think that animal acts in a circus are either commendable
or the highest point of animal evolution.) I do not believe
that if I was rude to my mother-in-law I'm going to be
reborn as a Greek donkey. I do believe that if I have lived
a life of deliberate cruelty to animals I may well choose to
project my consciousness into an animal for a time, to
understand exactly what it feels like. Perhaps in the past
we did incarnate into animal bodies as part of our
progression towards a human body, and in fact some
regressions have brought up memories of clawed feet,

feathers and fur, but I do not believe we go back from humans to animal form again. However, in the book *The Only Planet of Choice* Phyllis Schlemmer and Palden Jenkins say that dolphins of today are the reincarnation of Atlantean scientists of yesterday. Having swum with dolphins in Australia and experienced their incredible intelligence, sensitivity and joy, I can well believe this is possible.

In Atlantis scientists, through misusing their knowledge, contributed to the downfall of the Atlantean civilisation. Perhaps today, in dolphin form, these same scientists now share their knowledge to help mankind evolve into the 21st century. We have certainly developed new systems of radar, telepathy and healing from dolphin contact.

Atlantis existed many centuries ago, so where have these scientists been and what have they done meanwhile? Perhaps they visited other planets in the solar system, interspersed with occasional incarnations on earth as farmers, housewives, delivery men or politicians. Maybe only now is the time right to clear their Karma.

Soygal Rinpoche, author of *The Tibetan Book of Living and Dying*, says: 'Karma does not ever become inoperative. It cannot be destroyed by time, fire or water. Its power will never disappear until it is "ripened".' In other words, Karmic time is either right or ripe when we are ready to meet it.

I found these words of Soygal Rinpoche awesome and slightly frightening. They took me back to my 16-year-old fear of vengeful deities waiting to pounce on me for indiscretions long forgotten. I then remembered another spiritual teacher who told me that guilt causes Karma. (So no guilt, no Karma.) At the time I found this difficult to accept and understand, but on reflection I realised that guilt attaches us, more strongly than glue, to people and events.

Edgar Cayce said: 'Karma is rather the lack of living up to that which "ye know ye should do",' which implies that Karma is a matter of our own conscience, and so again of guilt.

To feel no guilt would mean total, unconditional love and acceptance of ourselves and therefore for others, love for *all* our parts – from the meanest and most vindictive to the glorious and most altruistic – without any judgement or qualification. For most of us this is virtually impossible but, if so, it brings us under the Law of Grace, which supersedes the Law of Karma and erases all karmic debts.

Beinsa Douna, the great Bulgarian spiritual master, mystic and teacher, sometimes known as Peter Deunov, taught that to dedicate one's life to spiritual growth and service to others also erases Karma. Again, by so doing we bring grace into our lives.

Edgar Cayce's readings said that the manner in which to meet Karma was through forgiveness. 'As ye would be forgiven so forgive others.' Forgiveness has always been a major part of spiritual growth. A simple affirmation of forgiveness which I use myself is: 'Through the divine in me, I forgive the human in you and in me, which caused whatever the problem is or was.' It bypasses the personality which says, 'I won't, or I can't forgive', and invokes grace into the situation. For me it always works.

The 20th century has introduced us to an accelerated life-style. Just as we have instant news, food or coffee, so we now have instant Karma. For example, Tom got into a fight in his local pub and thoroughly thrashed two men. He went home and walked into a low-hanging beam which knocked him out and gave him a black eye. Whatever we do, think, feel or imagine may rebound almost immediately.

Karma may initially dismay us when we meet the consequences of our actions face to face. However, Karma is not a predetermined fate, nor is there a previously structured response that we are expected to conform to. It provides continual opportunity to try and try again, and gives spiritual significance to what otherwise might be haphazard and meaningless events. The Law of Continuity in Action, or Karma, describes a sort of chain reaction – like throwing pebbles into a pond – in which the result itself will eventually become a future cause.

Karma is a form of cosmic dance in which we dance to our own, not someone else's, tune. It shows us that our soul's journey through time is always guided by choice. We have the free will to choose our response to whatever happens at any single moment of the day or night. We are free to act or react, to create our own solutions. Each life is an expression of the soul's creativity. (Some must have a great sense of humour!) and will ultimately lead to spiritual responsibility and enlightenment.

If the word Karma still inspires dread and a sense of 'I must now take life very seriously', remember the monk who asked his teacher what he should do to clear his Karma, become a better monk, and reach enlightenment. His master replied: 'Did you eat breakfast today?' 'Yes,' said the monk. 'Well then, wash your bowl.' The monk was enlightened.

3

THE
AKASHIC
RECORDS

Ask, and it shall be given you; seek, and ye shall find;
knock, and it shall be opened unto you.

MATTHEW, 7:7

Sachindra Majundar (*Yoga Principles and Practices*) says
that life is like a game of bridge in which we cannot
change the cards we have been dealt, but how we play our
hands depends on us. Therefore whether we play the
game well or badly, use our opportunities or miss them,
depends on the knowledge we have both of ourselves and
of the game. If this is so, how can we arrive at this
knowledge?

In 1972 a hypnotised man jerked violently, as if hit in
the solar plexus by an unseen force, and suddenly began
to speak in a stern and powerful voice. The young and
inexperienced hypnotist was rigid with shock as he
listened to the following words emanating not from the
mouth of his subject, but from his stomach: 'You have not
attained sufficient growth of spiritual awareness to understand contacts with these records. That which you
perform is a foolish experiment, for you attempt to

harness powers you do not understand, and to contact sources, records and intelligence you are not familiar with!'

The hypnotised man was Paul Solomon. The records that he, via the hypnotist, had inadvertently tapped into were the Akashic records. The word Akasha, or Akasa, is Sanskrit, meaning the etheric, electro-magnetic, spiritual substance of the universe, upon which is recorded every single thought, word and deed since the beginning of time.

The Akashic record suggests the mind and memory of God – an archetypal record of everything that has ever happened, a library of universal knowledge containing limitless information on any and every subject, including each individual's soul record of other lives.

In fact, Paul's own experience while hypnotised was like a dream in which he drifted up a green hill and into an enormous temple-like building in which there was a vast library. As he reached to take a book from the shelf his panic-stricken hypnotist woke him. However, like Edgar Cayce, who said that the Akashic records were to the mind what cinema was to the physical world, he later went on to give many readings.

During each reading he went back to the same library. Only when he found and opened the book recording the soul life of each person who consulted him was he able to provide the answers and information requested. He was also shocked at the similarity of so many lives, and said: 'With so much opportunity (in this and other lives) to change and grow, why don't we?'

Divining The Akashic Records

Three or four thousand years ago shamans in China took tortoise shells and dropped them into the fire. The cracked patterns that then emerged on the shells were used as a source of divination. They were 'read' to analyse past and present, as well as to predict the future. Primitive tribes communicated with trees, animals, birds and flowers. They cast bones or stones, listened to crystal skulls, gazed at the drifting shapes of clouds or into the sky to learn their history. In Greece and Egypt the Oracles were consulted daily. Students in the Schools of the Mysteries were taught to investigate their soul records, not just to understand their present existence, but also to prepare for their next.

In Sri Lanka, the tiny island at the tip of India where I was born, soothsaying, in various forms, was a normal part of daily life. Friends once took me to see an astrologer of high repute – he advised the government. He looked into my eyes for a long time, and then moved his fingers through a pile of sand which lay on the desk in front of him. Gazing at the patterns in the sand, he proceeded to tell me facts about myself, my life and my family which were all completely accurate.

From the dawn of time we have used countless methods of divination. We have sat in a witch-doctor's hut in Africa, and at the feet of an Indian sage. We have visited mediums and clairvoyants in Battersea or three doors down the road (who may or may not produce ectoplasm as proof of their connection with other planes). We have gazed into crystal balls, examined tea-leaves and formations of coffee grains. We have studied astrology, tarot, runes, numerology, the I Ching. In all cases our main aim is the same: to contact a superior source of intelligence who (we hope) will tell us what to do.

This superior source is the Akashic Records. It is described by Jung as the collective unconscious, by Cayce as a river of thought (accessible to anyone prepared to develop spiritual or psychic faculties), by Joan Grant as

Far Memory, and by W. B. Yeats as a Great Memory which passes from generation to generation.

Paul Solomon's voice, when asked: 'Who are you?' replied: 'I am the source of Paul's intelligence, part of his consciousness from the beginning of time.' The voice added that this intelligence was available to everyone. In other words, we do not have to be highly intelligent, psychic, clairvoyant or telepathic to be in touch with this intelligence, but rather more open to asking questions, maybe through prayer, and listening to the answers, maybe through meditation. As the Bible suggests, to ask is to receive, to knock is to open doors or windows of our minds in order to allow whatever answers we need to flow in.

Maybe we should try to emulate Buddha, who said:

I remembered many, many former existences I had passed through; one, two births, three, four, five, fifty, one hundred. A hundred thousand in various world periods. I knew everything about these various births, where they had taken place, what my name had been, which family I had been born into, and what I had done. I lived through again and again the good and bad future of each life, and my death in each life, and came to life again and again. In this way I recalled innumerable previous existences with their exact characteristics, features and circumstances. This knowledge I gained in the first watch of the night.

We do not have to be highly evolved Buddhas to begin to ask for information that will inevitably change our lives. Dreams, meditation, visualisation, imagination, intuition and relaxation are all keys to learning to read the records. Déjà-vu, hunches, sudden insights, flashes of inspiration are like earthquake cracks that open for a second and give us brief glimpses into our own knowing.

Déjà-vu literally means 'already seen', and is used to describe the sudden eerie sense of 'I've been, seen, or done this before'. It intimates the idea of pre-existence. For example, during World War II the American general, George Patton, arrived in the French town of Langres. When a French officer suggested he show the general around, Patton replied: 'You don't have to. I know this place well.' He then proceeded to lead the officer all over Langres and, though he had never been there before, included a detailed tour of the Roman ruins. Before his death, General Patton wrote a poem called 'Through a Glass Darkly', in which he not only revealed his belief in many lives, but also claimed that in many of his he had been a warrior.

The Soul's Journey

In later chapters I describe some simple but effective exercises that can help us delve into our past – and maybe even our future – history. Meanwhile it is important to remember that we ourselves are the only ones who truly know the A to Z of our soul's journey through time and space – even though most of us do not believe, or have forgotten that we do.

Many times man lives and dies.
Whether man dies in his bed
Or the rifle knocks him dead,
A brief parting from those dear
Is the worst man has to fear.
Though grave-diggers' toil is long,
Sharp their blades, their muscles strong,

They but thrust their buried men
Back in the human mind again.

WILLIAM BUTLER YEATS, *Under Ben Bulben*

We forget so much of what happens in this life, even from one week to the next, that it is hardly surprising that we forget the details of other lives. Plato described this memory lapse as the result of imbibing from the cup of Lethe, or drinking the waters of forgetfulness. Gandhi said it was nature's kindness that we did not remember countless births, as the burden would be too much, and Gustav Mahler wrote that: 'We all return, and it does not make the slightest difference whether or not we remember the former life.' For Mahler what mattered was what we did with each life.

If in the past it was nature's kindness to allow us to live like sleepwalkers with amnesia, it is now that same kindness that gives us the shake-up to wake-up. Many of us need the drama of loss or disaster to jolt us awake. The general global upheavals – wars, strikes, political unrest, holes in the ozone layer, storms, earthquakes, volcanic eruptions, the loss of health, wealth and work, have forced many of us to review our lives. The explosion of interest in spirituality and alternative medicine has stimulated awareness that we are not mere physical creatures moving from birth to death, but spiritual creators of our own reality. It is a major shift of identity.

All is impermanent in man except the pure bright essence of Alaya – the Universal Self. Man is its crystal ray, a beam of light immaculate within, a form of clay material upon the lower surface. Thy shadows (or bodies) live and vanish, that which in thee shall live forever, that which in thee *knows*, for it is knowledge, is not of fleeting life; it is the Man that was, that is, and will be, for whom the hour shall never strike.

The Voice of the Silence (Tibetan Buddhist Scripture)

Part of that shift needs to encompass the idea that we are the sum total of all our parts – including the bits and pieces of past-life personalities that, consciously or unconsciously, may still affect this life. To become perfectly whole (not wholly perfect) we need to integrate these parts. Without knowing what they are, how can we?

In earlier centuries, we played our parts in life like an actor on a stage who, if distracted by other roles, would forget his current lines. Today, in order to give our best performance, and audition for the next, we are forced by life to review our previous roles, to see the whole picture and not just a fragment of it, to become conscious directors and producers of our dramas, instead of unconscious bit-players in them. In this way we take control, acquire power and assume responsibility for the production in hand, instead of blaming others for it if it is not a box-office success.

Akasha And Astrology

Today may be one of our best times for this search. Astrologically, the current influence of Pluto suggests that we have never had greater opportunities to discover our pasts than we do now. Pluto, known as the Lord of the Underworld and the planet of re-birth, speeds up man's awareness of reincarnation and Karma. In the 1990s this can be seen by the hundreds of films, books, magazine columns, newspaper articles and television programmes devoted to subjects that range from psychic phenomena, near-death experiences, and channelling to before-, between-, and after-lives – all reflections of the occult explosion into a new era. (Occult adventures are the name of the game when Pluto comes to town, especially when Pluto is in transit with Scorpio, as it is now, and will be until November 1995.)

Pluto symbolises descent into the underworld, the downward spiral of spirit into matter, which brings about confrontation with our darkest, most hidden parts, both from this and our other lives. Pluto forces us to face old, non-productive patterns of behaviour, and to let them go, and therefore it introduces us to multitudinous deaths within one lifetime.

This descent into the underworld is similar to the story of Beauty and the Beast. Beauty, when confronted by the ugliness of the Beast, faces her own shadow, the sum total of all that is repressed and denied in her; old wounds, feelings, fears, failures, restricting beliefs, ideas and prejudices. Through this confrontation, Beauty finally accepts and loves all that she is, and so transforms the Beast into a handsome prince.

Pluto in Scorpio means the lower self must die, or give way to the higher. This is why so many lives and institutions not based on absolute truth are crumbling around us now. Anything corrupt, criminal or false – individually or collectively – is under tremendous pressure. Computer research shows that some of the world's most cataclysmic events happened during the Pluto/Scorpio ages. When I lived in America I knew Isabel Hickey, a well-known astrologer, who said that Pluto's transit through Scorpio would eliminate ancient wrongs and evils by 'stimulating a purge never before seen in the world'.

While Pluto promotes death of the old and birth of the new, Saturn is associated with Karma, and is sometimes called the Grim Reaper or the Lord of Karma. According to astrologer Liz Greene, Saturn is 'connected with the educational value of pain'. Saturnian lessons usually come through loss, depression or illness, and are likely to hit us most during the years of our Saturn return (when Saturn has completed its first cycle of the zodiac since our birth).

Astrology is a scientific study of the planets and the stars and how their movements interrelate with life on earth. It is an ancient system which shows us our patterns of re-birth and Karma, and also says that we are not the way we are *because* of our star signs, but that the way we *are* drew us into the energy field of those particular configurations.

The ebb and flow of planets and stars within our solar system indicate certain energies available to us, but do not compel us to use or to conform to them. Because, however, the planetary energies for the 1990s suggest we have unique opportunities completely to clear all individual and world Karma, we would be mad not to avail ourselves of them.

A personal horoscope, when properly interpreted, is similar to an Akashic reading. It outlines strengths and weaknesses inherited from the past, points out paths and possibilities available to us, as well as pitfalls to avoid, and suggests how we can best achieve our fullest potential.

Dreams

Another way of contacting the Akashic records is through dreams. A dream is the soul assessment of how well (or not) we deal with the day-to-day challenges of our lives. This assessment is then recorded on the Akasha and reflected back to us through dream images and stories. Even when the dreams are of the past (of this or other lives) or the future, they only come at a particular moment when we need to incorporate the relevant memory or information into today's life.

A fairly dramatic example of this is Peter's dream, which came two days after he was diagnosed as having cancer. His doctor told him the only treatment was major surgery and chemotherapy. Peter's father, with whom he had always had a difficult relationship, had died six months previously. In his dream Peter saw himself as a Viking battling against the authority of his chief, who finally caused Peter's death. He saw in his dream that even today he still seethed (unconsciously) with resentment towards the Viking chief who became his father. His father's death then triggered this resentment, which appeared to be the cause of the cancer. This understanding enabled him, awake, to forgive both the Viking and his father. The cancer subsequently disappeared, without surgery or chemotherapy.

The spirit of man has two dwelling places, both this world and the other world. The borderline between them is the third, the land of dreams . . .

UPINASHADS

Ann Ree Colton, an American clairvoyant, spiritual teacher and author of many books, says that to dream of turquoise means that the dreamer is initiated into the World Akashic records, where he can understand the different stages of evolution. Also, to dream of fabric that in some way restrains physical movement means we are raising our consciousness to a level of Akashic understanding. She adds that if we can master the lower planes (the lower self) we gain the ability and power to research the Akasha far more easily.

Interpreting The Akashic Records

In other words, to read the Akashic records accurately, we must free our spiritual vision from distraction by the physical senses. Short-term, this means meditation, a prayer, an affirmation such as: 'I do this to communicate with the God in me – the highest in me'; or, 'Let nothing that is not of God approach me now.' Long-term, it means working on ourselves so that we are in control of all our senses, and not controlled by them.

The universe is thought itself, existing on many levels of vibration, from the finest to the most dense. Our own vibratory rate will draw us to the planes or levels that we are in harmony with, just as it draws to us, like a magnet, people and situations of the same vibration. If we can lift our vibratory rate, we also lift our consciousness to a level where negativity cannot affect us. It is a little like a fan which when switched off, is a set of solid visible metal blades, easy to touch. When switched on, it becomes almost invisible, and certainly untouchable.

The true Akashic records exist in the highest, finest levels of vibration. To attune to them, we need to be in spiritual harmony with them. Another level of Akasha is like a reflection or projection of the original Akasha on the etheric. Many psychics, mediums and clairvoyants interpret from these records, using psychic rather than spiritual vision. It is similar to seeing an image of a garden reflected on the glass of a window, or the blurred imprint of a photograph negative instead of the photograph itself. In both cases what one sees makes everything look back to front, and therefore subject to misinterpretation. In addition the Akasha, as I mentioned earlier, contains not just the intent, event and result, but also the soul's assessment of all three – to say nothing of how our personal Akasha relates to that of the planet.

Accurate readings depend on the inner development and spiritual evolution of the reader. Which does not mean that we cannot learn to do this ourselves.

Another point to remember is that a strong personality, and/or a memorable life, leaves a stronger imprint on the electro-magnetic spiritual substance from which the Akasha is formed. This means that people who tap into this imprint en route to their own records (so to speak) will sometimes identify themselves with this or that character.

In the course of my life I have met at least nine Henry VIIIs, a dozen or so Mary Queen of Scots and Queen Elizabeth Is, quite a large number of Nefertitis, Ahkenatens, Ramses I, II, and IIIs, Cleopatras and Queen of Shebas, interspersed with Mary Magdalenes and a variety of disciples, and of course many others. Each had been told by different psychics, and I'm sure in good faith: 'You were A, B, or C.' There was no question in any of these people's minds about the truth of what they had been told. In fact, during a visit to Los Angeles, twelve women in the course of one day, each separately told me in hushed tones: 'I want you to be the first to know! I was the Virgin Mary.' No matter how important they might have been in the past, the only relevance now is, what are they here to do today?

In fairness to the twelve Virgin Marys, the Essenes trained twelve girls to be possible mothers to the Messiah when they knew He was due to arrive. It is possible that each woman I spoke to had a previous life as one of these twelve, and mistook herself for the real Mary. It is also possible for us to have what is called a 'seed-atom' connection to a past-life personality, rather as my great-great-grandchildren might say: 'I was Soozi Holbeche.' It would be true that in a sense they would be a part of me, but no one of them would be my whole personality.

Another confusion can arise if, for example, someone lives a life in close proximity to an important person. Thus if I had spent years as lady-in-waiting to Queen Victoria in a past life, I might well today mistake her identity as mine.

Crossing The Boundaries

However daunting this may sound, I have found that the individual or group past-life therapy sessions, in which each person does his own reading, albeit with guidance, allows him to discover his own truth. The urgent *need* to know, rather than mere curiosity, helps to bring this about – plus, when we do it for ourselves, we have a direct line to our own inner wisdom. Often when true memory comes to the surface there is a strong emotional and/or physical reaction which subsequently leads to a change in lifestyle, attitude or even physical healing. When we use an outside agent it is like making a call to America via the telephone exchange instead of by direct dialling. In the former case there are probably greater chances of getting a crossed line or static interference that makes it impossible to understand what is being said.

In the world today there are literally hundreds of men and women who claim to mediate between visible and invisible worlds as 'channels'. Some of them give us fascinating and valuable information, usually through contact with a discarnate entity or an extra-terrestrial. In fact, discarnate communication is so popular, especially in America, that many channellers have their own television programmes.

Instead of thinking that these channels are in some way superior or more spiritually evolved than we are, we should see the current channelling epidemic as indicative of a 'rending of the veil' – a melt-down of the barriers – between physical and spiritual consciousness, not just for the channellers, but for all humanity. This means that the information that can tell us exactly what to do as the 20th century gives way to the 21st is available to us all, if we are willing to ask for it. As I quoted from Matthew at the beginning of the chapter, 'Ask, and it shall be given you; seek, and ye shall find; knock and it shall be opened unto you.'

Discarnate communication is part of the enormous and extraordinary transformation taking place on the planet today. In my previous book, *Awakening to Change*, I look at this in detail. We are crossing boundaries between the known and the unknown, making a quantum leap from self to cosmic consciousness. While some of us feel there was never a more exciting time to be alive – even the molecular structure of our physical bodies is changing to adapt to the new frequencies flooding the planet – others feel insecure and afraid.

If we feel insecure, instead of trusting ourselves, we tend to run to others for information. To run to others means we are not taking responsibility for our lives. We literally give our power away.

Children of the future will read their Akashic records and review their past lives almost as we watch serial plays on television. Today most of us have to put a little effort into it.

A wonderful, and simple, way to begin is to study the shape, height, health, likes, dislikes, strengths, weaknesses and tendencies built into our physical bodies. A body, like an artist's painting, is a unique expression of imagination and creativity. It is a living record of everything that has ever happened to it. Eyes, hands, feet – even teeth – all have stories to tell that can be read and analysed.

Every cell, muscle, tissue, as well as the bones and

systems of the body, contain memory. Cells and molecules
are born and die continuously. When new cells are born
into a particular matrix of thought and emotion, they
hold that memory. Thus every new cell carries the new
memory as well as duplicating previous memories handed
on by old cells. In this sense, each cell resembles a
miniature Akashic record. The aura (the electro-magnetic
field around the body) and the chakras (the energy centres
that go from the top of the head to the base of the spine)
also contain vital information. This is why many therapists when doing various types of bodywork pick up or
diagnose the *source* of a patient's problems, instead of the
symptom.

We can do the same for ourselves. We do not have to be
psychic to 'read' or find meaning in what is written into
our bodies, auras and chakras. We merely have to study
them.

There are as many different ways of tapping into our
own Akashic records as there are foods on a restaurant
menu. We can take inner routes, via meditation, past-life
therapy, dreams, visualisation exercises, or outer routes
via bodywork, astrology, runes, tarot, or I Ching. All we
need to remember is that learning to read the Akasha is
similar to learning a foreign language. With practice,
patience and perseverance, anyone can do it.

As Saint Thomas Aquinas said: 'Recognise what is
before your eyes, and what is hidden will be revealed to
you.'

4

SUGGESTED CASES FOR REINCARNATION

I firmly believe, and this belief is based on investigation, observation and, in a measure, personal experience – that somehow, somewhere and sometime, we return in another human form, to carry on, as it were, through another lifetime, perhaps through many succeeding lifetimes, until some strange destiny is worked out to its ultimate solution.

HARRY HOUDINI (1874–1926)

Cases From India

On June 2nd 1961, Gurdeep Kaur, the young mother of four children, was murdered by her husband in India.

Seven years later Reena Gupta, not even two years old, told her grandmother: 'I have a very bad husband – he killed me.' Reena went on to describe in detail her previous family, which included four children she claimed were hers. On family outings Reena, so young she could barely walk, stared at people in the street, looking, as she explained when asked, 'for my *gharwala* (husband) and children'.

Confused, amazed, and even annoyed by their daughter's

bizarre behaviour – especially when she criticised the way her mother cooked and ran the house – the Guptas rejected Reena's utterances as pure fantasy and imagination. However, a friend, familiar with the idea of reincarnation, was intrigued enough to investigate Reena's story.

These investigations eventually led to a meeting with Gurdeep Kaur's parents. When Reena saw them for the first time she exclaimed with delight: 'They are my mother and father!' Later she met and recognised Gurdeep's sister as well as Gurdeep's four children – all of whom she greeted with great joy and excitement.

Later still, when she was nine years old, Reena was brought face to face with Surjeet Singh, the man who was both husband and murderer of Gurdeep. After ten years in gaol, he was released for good behaviour. When Reena saw him she shrank back, saying: 'He will kill me again!'

Titu was two and a half years old when he began to speak about his 'other' family. He described shops he owned in Agra (India) that sold electronic equipment such as radios, television sets, record players and sound systems. Having seen Titu on video I can vouch for the fact that, even very young, he looked and spoke like a 40-year-old business man. Like Reena Gupta, Titu claimed that he was murdered, 'and my business conned away from me'.

When asked about his 'other' family, Titu became very agitated and said: 'I must go and find my wife and sons, who are no doubt upset by my death.' Initially Titu's family ignored the child's statements, and even thought he was mad, but his anguish was so great that finally his grandfather took him to see the local sage, who said: 'Titu is completely sane. He remembers another life. What he suffers now, and even then, is part of his Karma.'

After months of anxiety on the part of Titu's current

family, they decided to 'lay the ghost to rest' by taking him to Agra. As they entered the town Titu became increasingly excited. He pointed out landmarks and streets, as well as the shops he claimed once to have owned. When taken into the main store, of which the other shops were branches, Titu approached the counter and greeted his 'wife' Uma. He was now about six years old. Titu asked Uma if she recognised him, and of course she said 'No'. He pointed to a photograph of Uma's dead husband, pinned to the wall and encircled with flowers, and again asked her if she knew who he was. Bewildered, Uma shook her head. Titu then asked her if she remembered a secret outing to a fair, at which her husband had bought her sweets. He also described his death, saying he was shot in the head as he returned home from work. Uma burst into tears, but later confirmed everything Titu said.

When Titu asked after his sons Uma, partly as a test of identity, suggested he should go to their school and pick them out. Titu arrived during a break and found the playground a seething mass of frenetic children. Within seconds, he identified his two sons, now older than he was, and accompanied them home to Uma. When they arrived together, Uma collapsed. She finally accepted that Titu was the reincarnation of her dead husband, but said: 'What am I to do? He is a child, I am middle-aged. I shall be happy to see him, but he now has another life.'

Titu's sons, when he told them he was their father, asked: 'Why are you smaller than us?' Titu replied: 'I died, and was born again.' They looked him up and down, and said: 'If you drink more milk you'll grow bigger.'

In America I heard a story about another Indian man. When taking a bath with his three-year-old son Bishen, he was suddenly asked: 'Do you have a mistress?' Taken aback, he listened while his son described the benefits a mistress could provide. 'You could sip champagne and smoke a cigar while she massaged your feet. A mistress brings you joy and helps you relax.'

Years later, Dr Ian Stevenson helped trace Bishen's memories back to the life of Laxmi Narayan, who died in 1918. Laxmi, son of a wealthy man, had indulged himself in everything money could buy – good food, clothes, wine and women. He had also fallen in love with a prostitute called Padma.

When Bishen was 23, he suddenly met and recognised Padma. He fainted. Recovered, Bishen, so far a strict teetotaler, rushed off, bought some wine, and went to Padma's house. There he proposed that they resume their old relationship. She pushed him away. 'Don't be ridiculous!' she exclaimed. 'I'm old enough to be your mother!'

Gopal, a poor, uneducated Hindu, suddenly remembered a past life in a province hundreds of miles from his current home. Gopal, now middle-aged, had never before left the village in which he was born, but to the astonishment of his neighbours, he set off to revisit his old haunts. Initially confused by the changes – he described everything as 'the same yet not the same' – he then began to recognise old landmarks. He finally discovered the ruins of his old home, and cried when he saw the fallen-in roof and crumbling walls.

When the oldest men in the village were questioned, they all remembered that, as boys, they had known that this house had been occupied by an old man with the same name Gopal had said was his in his previous life. While walking around the ruins, Gopal pointed to a particular spot and said: 'I buried a pot of silver there.' When the ground was dug up, there sure enough was an old pot containing silver coins.

> The Vedantic religion is more logical when it teaches
> that the suffering is a consequence, than the
> Christian religion that says it is a precedent. The
> effect cannot be precedent of the cause ... Nobody
> suffers innocently. Neither the suckling. Just the
> innocently looking suckling proves that our life on
> the earth is the consequence of a former life.
>
> GEZE GARDONYI

Mother, I'm Coming Back

In 1957, Dr Leslie Weatherhead, a well-known Methodist
minister, gave a lecture in London entitled 'The Case for
Reincarnation'. During this lecture he said: 'The intelligent Christian asks not only that life should be just, but
that it shall make sense. Does the idea of reincarnation
help here? I think it does.' An objector from the audience
cried out: 'If what you say is true, I should lose my
identity in repeated incarnations.' Dr Weatherhead
replied: 'I don't think you will, any more than you have
lost it already a dozen times. For example, you are the
little, runny-nosed Willie Tomkins who got punished for
being late at school. Do you want to identify with him?
You are the Will Tomkins who wrote wet verses and
slipped them into the hand of a sixteen-year-old girl with
blonde plaits. Do you want to assert your identity with
him? You are the William Tomkins who was sacked for
being unable to account for money received on behalf
of your firm. Do you feel robbed if he passes out of
your sense of identity? You are W. Tomkins, with
rheumatic joints, poor sight and hearing, whose body is
now a nuisance ... Is it really important that the whole

personality of Tomkins should go on for a hundred, a thousand, ten thousand, a hundred thousand years – still as William Tomkins?'

Dr Weatherhead then told the following story. An Italian couple, the Battistas, were the proud parents of a daughter named Blanche. The Battistas employed a Swiss nannie, Marie, who taught Blanche to sing a French lullaby. Sadly, Blanche died, and Marie returned to Switzerland. Three years later Blanche's mother became pregnant. During the pregnancy she had a waking dream in which she heard Blanche say: 'Mother, I'm coming back!'

When the new baby was born she resembled Blanche in every way, so they called her Blanche also. Nine years after the death of their first daughter, they were shocked to hear the French lullaby she used to sing floating out from the nursery of Blanche No. 2, who was now nearly six years old. They opened the door, and were amazed to see Blanche No. 2 sitting bolt upright in bed and singing the lullaby in perfect French. 'What are you doing?' exclaimed the mother. 'How do you know that song?' Blanche No. 2 replied: 'I'm singing a French song. I've always known it!' Yet from the moment of Blanche No. 1's death, everyone had scrupulously avoided speaking a word of French in the house.

Waking Visions

In 1978 I met Sylvia Cranston, compiler and editor of many books on reincarnation. She told me the following two stories. The first was about a young American girl who had terrifying waking visions in which she saw two huge yellow cats tearing to pieces, then eating, someone called Marcella. Throughout her childhood she was tormented by these visions.

Years later, now married and living in Rome, she met a woman at a dinner party who seemed so familiar she could not stop staring at her. As they left the table the woman approached her and said: 'Don't you remember me? I was Marcella, and you saw me torn to pieces in the arena by lions. I felt sure I would meet you again in this incarnation.'

O youth or young man, who fancy that you are neglected by the Gods, know that if you become worse you shall go to worse souls, or if better to the better, and in every succession of life and death you will do and suffer what like may fitly suffer at the hands of like. This is the justice of heaven, which neither you nor any other unfortunate will ever glory in escaping . . .

PLATO, *Laws, Book X*

The second story also began with recurring childhood visions and dreams. In them a young boy called Peter (not his real name) saw himself as an officer commanding troops at a camp site by a river. Wandering along the river bank, he found a house, and inside it a beautiful woman. He seized her and dragged her back to the camp, where she died of a broken heart. As she died she cursed him, saying that one day he would wear his uniform as a mockery, and would also beg her for food.

As a man, Peter became a bit of a drop-out, glad to do any odd job that came his way. One such job was that of an extra in the film *Ben Hur*. As he put on his costume of kilt, tunic, helmet, sword and shield, he was shocked to realise they were identical to the uniform in his dream. Much later, on a visit to England (where he was astounded to discover the site of his dream camp) he knocked on a door to ask for food. The woman who opened it stared at him in horror. 'Go away!' she screamed. Instantly Peter recognised her as the woman from his dream.

Important Research

Dr Ian Stevenson is now considered to be one of the world's leading authorities on reincarnation. When he began his investigations, he was chairman of neurology and psychiatry at the University of Virginia. Because many of his subjects were Asian, Indian or Sri Lankan, he left his job in order to free himself to travel anywhere in the world at a moment's notice. After interviewing hundreds of people, many of them children, he wrote a book, *Twenty Cases for Reincarnation*, which has become almost a classic for those interested in the subject. Dr Stevenson says he became intrigued with life after death, and survival through reincarnation, because heredity and environmental influences usually did not account for the personality as we see it.

Dr Stevenson described how 'in studying cases of reincarnation I have to use the method of the historian, lawyer and psychiatrist. I gather testimony from as many witnesses as possible.' Investigations of children who claim to have lived before frequently reveal that the last life ended violently. A violent death appears to cut short in-between-life time and speed re-birth. This means that many of the friends and relations of past-life personalities are still alive today to verify their claims. What better witnesses could there be?

In the East, life is held to be a journey through time, a journey that involves millions and millions of years. Palingenesis (from the Greek words for 'again'-birth), transmigration and samsara (continuous cycles of birth and re-birth) are accepted as a kind of cosmic dance with the creator. A child who remembers another life (whether as a beggar-woman scrubbing clothes in the Ganges, or a Spanish dancer clicking her castanets in a wild fandango, or a monk sitting on top of a mountain in Tibet, or a judge coldly dispensing justice in a grey court) is taken seriously and treated with respect. And this in spite of the superstition that children who remember past lives die young.

In the West, at least in the past, if a child said, 'I was Joe (or Josephine) Soap, and lived in Alaska catching fish', the tendency was either to smile indulgently and ignore such statements, or to snap and suppress them by saying: 'Stop it! Be quiet! It's only your imagination!'

Today, however, more and more children, especially in Western countries, are remembering past lives.

Chay, when three years old, was taken by his parents to a fireworks party. He became so hysterical when the fireworks popped and banged that they had to take him home. From then on, he could not bear loud noises. Even when a car backfired, Chay hid under his bed. Finally his mother took him to a therapist, who asked him to draw what he felt when he heard sharp, explosive noises. Chay drew a picture of soldiers encamped in a circle. The drawing included guns, horse-drawn wagons, and uniforms of a bygone era about which Chay, at three, could not possibly have had any conscious knowledge.

In response to questions from the therapist, Chay remembered being shot dead as a black soldier during the American Civil War. He described the terror of carrying a gun, hiding behind rocks, and shooting at anything that moved, as well as the pain of losing his wife and family.

Today Chay is pale-faced, red-haired and freckled. Through re-living his past (which was checked out by historians) he is no longer afraid of noise.

Caroline was so inordinately afraid of fire that her parents feared for her sanity. At two, three and four years old, she refused to go to bed unless with her favourite toys beside her. When she was eleven she awoke from a nightmare screaming: 'The house is on fire!' and ran downstairs, crying: 'I smell of smoke! I smell of smoke!' Seconds later, she saw herself as a Victorian girl (who was actually eleven years old) burned to death in a fire. After regression therapy Caroline too was cured of her phobia, though she does say: 'I still keep my favourite things under my bed. I'm packed and ready to go!'

Sophie, 18 months old and strapped into her baby-seat in the back of the family car, suddenly shouted to her mother as they approached a bridge: 'This is just like where I died! I was in my car!'

Astounded, Sophie's mother abruptly stopped the car. Sophie could barely talk, and yet now sounded like a mature woman. She continued: 'I could reach the pedals because I had longer legs then.' Sophie had never sat in the front seat, so could not possibly have known that a car had pedals. She went on to describe how her car went off the bridge and into the river, where she 'lay under water and nobody came'.

Ann, born five years after her grandfather's death, claimed to be the reincarnation of him. She knew all the details of his life, his pet name when a child (long forgotten by most of the family) his habits, likes and dislikes. She described how her grandfather was shot, and died from a bullet wound in the neck. Today Ann has a big lump in her neck in exactly the same spot where the bullet hit her grandfather. Initially incredulous, and after much investigation, Ann's family now accept that she is indeed her grandfather's reincarnation.

Strange lumps, bumps and scars often bear witness to

how a past-life personality died – especially when it was a violent death. One child, who claimed to have had his throat cut, was born in this life with a scar round his neck. Another described an attack in which a knife was thrust into his chest and dragged downwards to his stomach. He too was born with a jagged scar exactly like the wound of his description. Titu, whose story I told at the beginning of the chapter, has a purple birth-mark in the exact spot where the bullet hit him when he was Uma's husband.

In Dr Stevenson's research, he has frequently tracked down the medical records covering the death of the previous personality of whom a child has claimed to be the reincarnation. He has found that the position of wounds which caused the previous personality's death corresponds accurately with the descriptions which the child gave of it, as well as matching the position of the scars which the child currently bears. It is as if the child has so strongly integrated the traumatic memory of his past death that he uses his new body to say: 'Look what happened to me!'

During past-life therapy it is also quite common for various signs and symptoms to appear on or in the body. These can manifest in a rash, a bruise, severe pain, sweating, cramp, bones cracking, or limbs becoming locked in awkward positions. Fortunately, at the end of the therapy session these symptoms disappear.

Most early researchers into evidence for reincarnation used hypnosis to regress people into the memory of other lives. Full hypnosis bypasses the present personality, and often allows memories to arise that are so intense that it is like re-living rather than remembering. (I do not use hypnosis myself, but still find that the type of regression in which someone is fully conscious of his current identity, and yet has access to his past, allows the same 're-living' to take place.)

For Dr Stevenson, the best evidence of re-birth came from spontaneous recall rather than guided, hypnotic suggestion. On the other hand, for Peter Ramsder, an Australian hypnotherapist, the best evidence came from four women who under hypnosis and the watchful eye of television cameras, gave detailed descriptions of other lives which were then thoroughly investigated. The verification of their stories was made into a documentary and shown on Australian television in 1983. Hundreds of viewers wrote in, saying that this documentary had completely shattered their old and somewhat orthodox beliefs, and that reincarnation could be the only logical explanation.

Peter Ramsder's first subject, Cynthia Henderson, recalled a life in France. She described her husband, her life, and her children, as well as the château in which they lived. She spoke and understood French. Awake she did not.

Jenny Green remembered the life of Dorothy Helman, daughter of a Jewish jeweller, and a teenager in Dusseldorf when Hitler came to power. Hypnotised, she re-lived the fear of being chased and caught by the Nazis. 'We were taken to a village for Jews to live in. We cooked, cleaned, and washed the clothes of people who had gone. But where had they gone? Surely they wouldn't have left their clothes behind?'

She then talked about her friend Freda, who asked why the clothes kept coming. Now almost hysterical, Jenny, in trance, said: 'They took Freda. They beat her and kicked her. No questions. We must never ask questions. She just died in the dirt, and they wouldn't let us help.'

Gwen McDonald reverted to the life of Rose Duncan, born near Glastonbury in the 1700s. She described her upset when neighbours stole stones from the ruins of Glastonbury Abbey to strengthen the foundations of their own cottages. Her voice changed from Australian to a Somerset accent when she said: 'Yer shouldn't do that. It's all wrong.'

Helen Pickering, deep in trance, said: 'I am Dr James Archibald Burns. I hate the name Archibald. It was my father's name, and I never saw him laugh. He laughed with his drinking friends but he never laughed with me.' She then described her life as a highly respected doctor and Justice of the Peace in Blairgowrie, Scotland, in the 1830s.

When all the names, places and dates mentioned in these stories had been checked meticulously against old records and maps by impartial historians and independent witnesses, the women were flown from Australia to the scenes of their past lives. Their rising emotion when entering familiar countryside, their very real shock and tears when facing an old home (in Cynthia's case now a ruin) was, for the average viewer, far more convincing than a hundred academic arguments.

As Peter Ramsder said, it is more than fantasy, genetic memory or explanation of the psyche when each fact tallies with the physical reality.

All these stories strongly support the theory of reincarnation. In my next chapter I would like to show how the remembering of past lives can also heal.

5

MY INTRODUCTION
TO PAST-LIFE
THERAPY

I hold that when a person dies
His soul returns again to earth;
Arrayed in some new flesh disguise,
Another mother gives him birth.
With sturdier limbs and brighter brain
The old soul takes the road again.

JOHN MASEFIELD

Until I was in my twenties I had never heard of past-life or regression therapy.

My interest in general healing began when I was a child. If plants, animals or persons were ailing, I put my hands on or around them. A great heat, enough to make my hands tingle, flowed through me to them, and usually drew away the pain or sickness.

At the same time I 'saw' – from the centre of my forehead or Third Eye – through the current pain or problem to its root cause. (It was as if, in this moment, my Third Eye vision penetrated the so-called density of physical matter.) The root cause was usually an unresolved conflict, memory or feeling from the past, either from this or another life. I had no control over this seeing. It came and went as if an invisible switch went on or off in my brain. It also never occurred to me to share what I saw when this happened.

My interest in healing grew when, over the years, people around me (usually complete strangers) fainted, fell over, had epileptic fits, heart and asthma attacks, bleeding noses, broken ankles, and even went into premature labour. I held their hands and feet, stroked their hair, listened with deep interest to stories of domestic betrayal, scheming co-workers, errant children and careless doctors. Throughout I saw, on the inner screen of my mind, many of the other lives and personalities that set in motion what happened to these people in their present lives. I saw the connecting links, but had absolutely no idea how to help others to find these links for themselves.

I continued to care for and help others when the need arose. However, it was certainly not my main purpose. I pursued a variety of fairly colourful careers, in fashion, advertising, design, and finally theatre make-up. Two events then occurred which totally changed my life and pushed me into full-time healing and counselling. One was an NDE (near-death experience). The other was recovery from an accident which badly smashed my face. Initially I worked with accident victims, cancer patients, and the terminally ill. I shared with them everything I had done to put my own body and mind together, and from this my present healing practice gradually developed.

I taught meditation, visualisation, stress-release, journal-writing, dream, colour, sound and crystal therapy, together with other healing methods, but I never thought of guiding anyone into a past-life memory.

And then Pattie (not her real name) landed on my doorstep, and I was precipitated not just into past life or regression therapy, but also possession and exorcism.

Pattie

When Pattie erupted into my life I was tired. I had just finished a two-month visit to America, giving lectures and seminars, and I was anxious to get home. I was packing when Pattie burst into the room and begged me to help her. When I asked 'Why?' Pattie replied: 'I'm 34 years old. I've spent nearly half my life in a clinic and I can't go back there again!' (The clinic Pattie referred to used to be, and probably still is, well known for its treatment of people with severe psychiatric and psychological problems.) She told me that since she was twelve years old she had had recurring bouts of madness, which lasted for approximately six months. During these attacks she was hysterical and violent. She screamed, ranted and raved, used foul language (never heard in the house before!), threw china and furniture about, plastered the walls with food from her plate, tore up her clothes and ran down the road stark naked.

When Pattie was old enough to drive she used to drink three or four bottles of whisky and then roar down the local freeway in her car at top speed – a terror to other drivers and even the police when they chased her. Her family were also terrified by her sudden outbursts of uncontrollable behaviour, and they felt they had no option but to put her in a clinic (for her own sake as well as theirs) when they occurred.

In between attacks Pattie lived a relatively normal life, although always on tenterhooks for when the craziness might return.

When she came to me for help Pattie had just been forcibly removed from an aircraft. She had locked herself into the toilet for the duration of the flight in order, she said, 'to dress up as Archangel Gabriel. Gabriel told me to do this', she added. Minutes before landing, Pattie emerged to waft down the aisle in her angelic clothes, telling her fellow passengers to prepare for the hereafter as 'by tomorrow you will all be dead'.

At our first meeting, I simply stared at Patty aghast. Finally I said: 'I'm very sorry, but I can't help you. Even if I wanted to, your problems are way beyond my capacity and experience. Besides, I'm about to go back to London. You need professional help. You *must* see a qualified psychiatrist!'

Pattie reminded me that she had spent fifteen years all told under professional psychiatric care, and was still not cured. She also said that much of her treatment had consisted of drugs that had knocked her out for days on end. She described how she was often strapped into a straitjacket, or placed in isolation in a padded cell. 'I can't go back! There must be another way!' Maybe there was, I agreed, but certainly not with me.

Two hours later, on the strict understanding that I had no idea what to do, Pattie became my patient.

I think it would be marvellous if more and more people would become aware of the fact that there are many lives we have to live in order to learn all the lessons.

ELIZABETH KÜBLER-ROSS

It was now past midnight. Both of us aware of my imminent departure, we decided to begin at once. But how? I was far more concerned with the question of how to start than with anything else that might lead into.

Finally, in desperation, I said: 'Lie down!' And, because there was nowhere else, Pattie obediently stretched out on the floor. Not knowing what else to do, I lay down beside her, and silently prayed for help.

I suddenly felt as if my consciousness was inside Pattie's

mind and body. And not only inside her body but also inside an alien and powerful force that seemed to permeate her entire being. I found it extremely uncomfortable, and yet vaguely seductive, similar to the sense of floating away when an anaesthetic begins to take effect. A sickly sweet smell, almost like chloroform, pervaded the atmosphere around us.

It was an extraordinary, disconcerting, and painful experience. And yet it enabled me to ask questions I would never otherwise have thought to ask (from inside Pattie's own head, so to speak). In answering them, Pattie began to retrieve old memories, as well as the sensations and emotions associated with them. As a result, and throughout the night, she cried, screamed, howled and contorted her body into myriad grotesque positions.

I knew that Pattie was possessed. I was unsure whether her behaviour was her own, or induced by her possessing power. Neither did I feel, during our first session together, that it was appropriate to discuss possession.

Hours later I felt returned to my own body and, still lying side by side on the floor, we slept. I deferred my return to England and for five weeks, Pattie and I worked together in the same way every day.

During these five weeks we explored every year of Pattie's life. I discovered that when she was twelve she fell in love with Max, a favourite uncle. According to Pattie, Max, despite their many years' difference in age, also fell in love with her. They walked, talked, held hands together, and enjoyed each other's company until, when Pattie was 14 and Max 44, he died. Obsessed with his memory, Pattie kept every note, photo and memento of Max's life. Even now, Pattie told me, she spoke and wrote to Max as if he were still alive.

Prickles ran up and down my spine. I asked her if she ever sensed a not unpleasant but slightly suffocating energy around her. 'Oh yes, that's Max!' she replied.

When I suggested that her obsession for Max had drawn his spirit to her, and that for both their sakes she must now release him, she refused to do so.

Realising that Pattie was 12 when she fell in love and that was also when her periodic bouts of madness began, I asked her to close her eyes and tell me more about herself and her life at that age. 'I'm not twelve, I'm seven,' she replied. 'They're sending me away and I don't want to go.' Then, shouting at the top of her voice, she repeated: '*I don't want to go!*' while gesturing with her arms, as if pushing someone away. I assumed she meant she was being sent away to boarding-school, and asked her to describe it to me.

Suddenly her voice changed: 'I'm in the temple of Osiris. I'm a priestess training for initiation into the Mysteries. I'm learning to be a seer and an oracle. I'm not allowed to speak to anyone. I have to develop my inner vision without distraction.' Tears began to roll down her cheeks. She described how her family had sent her to the Temple, and she never saw them again.

Lonely and unhappy, Pattie (now re-living the life of Seshat) was frequently locked in a cell-like room, and given drugs to stimulate telepathy and clairvoyance. She contemplated suicide. On her twelfth birthday she was told she had advanced enough to undergo a major initiation, in which she was to be placed in a sarcophagus for three days and nights. This initiation symbolised death and re-birth. During it Seshat (Pattie) like other initiates, had to use her astral and spiritual bodies to explore other planes and realities.

After this ordeal, in which people sometimes died or went mad, the initiate had to describe to a priest everything he or she saw and experienced in different dimensions. (There is a similarity between this and the

American Indian vision quest. In Western culture, NDEs appear to be the replacement of this initiation.)

Frantic with fear, not only of the dark, silence and possible death, but also of the disgrace if she failed her test, Seshat escaped into insanity, and lost her place in the Temple. An older priest felt sympathy for her, and sometimes took her for walks around the Temple court-yards. When Seshat was 14 and the priest 44, he was summoned to the Pharaoh's court, and Seshat lost contact with him for ever. She lived another 30 or 40 years, then threw herself off a cliff.

As Pattie's story trailed to an end I said: 'Before you open your eyes, I want you to tell me if there is anyone from that other life who is part of your life today?' In a voice trembling with shock, Pattie said that the priest was now Max, her present family the reincarnation of her past family, and many of the doctors and nurses in the Menninger Clinic fellow-students, priests and priestesses in the Temple of Osiris.

We saw that her present life was an almost identical re-creation (though in modern terms) of her past. Even her experience of drugs and solitary confinement reflected aspects of her priestess's training.

Pattie recognised that her obsession with Max had started in this other life: 'He was the only person who deliberately sought me out, was kind and spent time with me after I lost my mind.' As Seshat, Pattie trusted him, and never recovered from his disappearance into the Pharaoh's court.

In today's life, Pattie's unconscious terror that madness would ensue if she failed a test actually triggered the madness. (It later transpired that when she was 12 she failed to pass entrance exams to a school previously attended by three generations of her family.) Her fear of losing her family, or anyone else she loved, also triggered her separation from them.

When Pattie emerged from this session she was very tired. But somehow the recognition and re-living of the life she described freed her from some of her old tension and anxiety. With a greater understanding of why she was the way she was, Pattie asked me to help her release Max.

I explained to Pattie that, having been suffused with Max's energy, and addicted to his presence, for so many years, she might feel lost and empty afterwards – as would a drug addict experiencing withdrawal symptoms. I told her that she must totally release Max for the duration of this life, and not attempt to hold even a fragment of his astral personality back. If and when she thought of him, she must do it as if popping a letter into a post-box. She must drop it in, walk away, and let it go.

After more fervent prayers for help, I told Pattie to lie down on the floor again. (Strangely, I never once thought of moving her onto a bed or cushions.) I surrounded her with crystals, flowers and candles, all of which helped to create a strong spiritual atmosphere. I spoke to Max as if he were physically present in the room. I told him that he was much loved, but that it was now time to move on. Pattie remained silent. Not knowing quite what else to do, I told Max he must 'follow the light', which would lead him to his proper place. I then called on angels, archangels, guides – and anyone else willing to do so – to help him. It seemed as if a voice in my ear whispered: 'He needs the Angels of the Purple Flame and the Angels of the Golden Nets,' so I called on them too.

After a few minutes we sensed Max lifting out of Pattie but still hovering over her. Until then I had knelt beside her. I now stood, and said three times in a loud, clear voice: 'In the Name of God I command you to be gone.' The atmosphere shivered and quivered around us, then cleared. An enormous peace enfolded us. The scent of roses filled the room. We prayed again and hugged each other.

Inexperienced as I was, I thought that we had healed the crux of Pattie's problems. In reality what we had solved was only the tiny tip of an iceberg which at times threatened to drown us both.

In the days ahead Pattie hit depths of despair and depression. She often exploded with rage, refused to get out of bed, would not eat or wash either herself or her clothes. I said: 'If you continue to behave like this, I'll smack your bottom!' And did. She threatened suicide so many times that I finally told her: 'I'm sick of this. Go ahead and do it!'

Despite these tantrums and setbacks, Pattie and I continued our daily work together. We delved into key events in Pattie's life, both good and bad, which often triggered the memories of other lives. When those other lives were acknowledged, healed and integrated, her symptoms of craziness began to recede.

Finally, bored with stories of dancing gypsies and onion-eating builders of pyramids or the Great Wall of China, I said: 'See if you can remember your conception, birth, and time in the womb.' Before I could ask any more questions, Pattie screamed and cried: 'I'm drowning! Water is suffocating me! I can't stay! I've got to go!' A few moments later she whispered: 'They don't want me. I shouldn't be there. I must go!'

In this session Pattie appeared to remember three attempts by her mother to abort her. The first was from jets of water squirted at high pressure into the womb. The second used a poisonous chemical or herbal concoction, which Pattie claimed had burned her. During the third attempt her consciousness opted out – and yet the baby survived and was born. Pattie hovered around, but never fully entered the baby's body.

Others did, however. I discovered eight lost souls who from time to time took over Pattie's body. It was at these times that Pattie became crazy. Following a similar process to the one in which we released Max, and over many days, we exorcised these eight entities, and created a space for Pattie's real essence to enter fully. (To do any form of exorcism, the exorcisers must be completely without fear, and be aware that the invading force needs as much help, compassion and understanding as does the possessed personality.)

Much later, we discovered that Pattie's family were related to her by Karma rather than blood. Pattie, although she did not know it when we worked together, was adopted. Her real mother did in fact try to abort her three times and finally, in desperation after her birth, left Pattie in an orphanage.

Pattie recovered completely, and never returned to the clinic. She is now a fully qualified and practising psychologist. It is largely thanks to Pattie, and to the case of the man that I shall now discuss, that much of the work that I do today is as it is.

Joost

Joost (not his real name) did not erupt into my life quite as had Pattie, but his impact was certainly similar.

About a week after my return to England from America, Joost telephoned me for an appointment. I was impressed that he was ready to fly from Amsterdam to London for it. He arrived at my address at 9AM, exactly on time. That mathematical precision was characteristic. At 44, he was a high-flying computer expert.

After a cup of coffee, I told him to lie on my bed. With great reluctance he did so. He made no move to take off his jacket or shoes first. To reassure him, I clasped his fully-shod foot in my hand. He jerked back, and nearly fell off the bed. Sensing his hatred of touch, I spent the next eight to nine hours touching him from head to foot. It was as if I were a blind man reading braille. Through my fingers I 'read' his life history. I told him what I had picked up and asked him to tell me if it was true or false. He verified it without exception. I also asked him to talk about his own experience of the events I described. Much of this led into his memory of past lives. In short, he was a typically emotionally repressed man who had armoured himself in his science. During the session I discovered that after a premature birth he had been put into an incubator. From then on his mother had been uneasy about touching him. He became so inhibited that he resisted any other woman touching him.

Although I already knew that touch was vital in healing and caring for people, I had never associated it as a way into the memories of this or past lives. When Joost finally departed into the night, I knew that from then on I must use this intuitive form of touch with everyone I treated. I should stress that my form of touch is a firm pressure from my fingertips searching for points of pain, rather than gentle massage. I always say a prayer, and go where my hands guide me.

Marian

My next client was a journalist doing an interview on NDE for a women's magazine. During our talk together the subject of reincarnation cropped up. She was fairly sceptical, and anyway more interested in present (i.e. early childhood) rather than past-life regression. However, she still asked me to 'do something with her'.

Slightly apprehensive, I laid her on my bed and began to push and prod into various parts of her anatomy. She claimed to have no deep-seated problems, phobias or fears, but wanted to 'test me out'.

A few minutes into the session, I asked her how she felt about disabled people – Down's Syndrome and cerebral palsied children in particular. She almost jackknifed off the bed, crying: 'How did you know?'

Marian, as I shall call her, then told me that she was in fact the mother of an illegitimate Down's Syndrome child. Although she worked hard to pay for the child's care, she refused publicly to acknowledge it, for fear of damaging her professional reputation, bringing down disrepute upon her parents (her father was a vicar), and losing any chance of making a decent relationship with a man. Marian, despite her protestations that 'there's nothing wrong with me', was riddled with guilt. I then decided to incorporate forgiveness – of self, and others – into my sessions.

As I continued my work, I discovered that every body I touched was like a finely-tuned computerised memory bank – a living record of its owner's life. I saw too that it was the *suppression* of the memories and emotions of certain events that created problems, rather than the *living experience* of the events themselves (no matter how traumatic) that did so. These repressed memories lock into our unconscious and cause physical, mental, and emotional difficulties. I found that pressure from my fingers not only released blocked physical energy, but also let the repressed feeling or trauma come to the surface. When something hidden or invisible surfaces, it no longer controls us.

I am sure that techniques such as acupressure or Rolfing have a similar effect today. However, my experiences occurred more than 20 years ago. It was thanks to

Pattie and Joost and other patients that I was then learning a form of spontaneous intuitive diagnosis.

A Therapeutic Approach

Initially, some patients preferred to go back through their present lives to their moments of birth, and no further. In this way many childhood traumas were healed. Others, who believed in reincarnation, or were open to the idea of it, were happy to go from present- to past-life regression. This usually resulted in a total transformation. When we understand why we act and react, we gain power. We move from victim to master.

As long as you are not aware of the continual law of Die and Be Again, you are merely a vague guest on a dark earth.

GOETHE

My use of past-life therapy is to help my patients tie up any loose ends or 'unfinished business' from previous lives that may still affect them in the present. This means that together we must thoroughly explore the lives that come up. In other words, in past-life therapy we do not simply find a life and say 'Oh, that's interesting!' then skip lightly on to the next one. We examine each past life exhaustively for its effect on the present one.

For 25 years I have used past-life therapy with hundreds of people all over the world. I shall describe some of their stories in my next chapter. Because each individual has his or her unique reasons for making an appointment, no two sessions are identical.

This is how my technique has evolved: I use quartz crystals, fresh flowers, candles and colours to create an atmosphere in which a person feels comfortable and relaxed. I now ask my patient to lie, not on the floor, but on a comfortable bed. (I find this better than a massage table, which tends to be a bit narrow.) I then surround him or her with crystals, because their energy is conducive to healing. Crystals stimulate the mind to be open and responsive, while they also help the body to relax.

I then light a candle and say a prayer in which I ask for the presence of angels and Masters of Light, to ensure that only what is appropriate for the highest good of the patient may take place. At the beginning of a session I sometimes play a meditational-type tape, as an aid to relaxation. I check the chakras, the energy points of the body, with my hand or with a crystal. Rather like a doctor taking a temperature before and after a treatment, I also check the chakras before and after a session. The difference confirms whether the healing has 'taken'.

I spend about 1–1½ hours pushing and prodding my patient's body. I work from head to toe, back and front. As I said earlier, I let my hands find their own way intuitively. At any point of physical pain I ask my patient to say aloud: 'I forgive myself.' This does not imply that he or she has committed a sin. It means, rather, that 'I give away, or release' what the body and mind unconsciously held onto.

The first half of the session concentrates on the patient's present life – from his or her current age back to birth, conception and pre-conception. It also examines the childhood relationships with parents, grandparents, siblings and friends to see how these helped to mould the present personality. It is very much a combined effort. I discuss what I am picking up, and constantly ask questions.

After an overview of the present life, we move into an exploration of others. We look for past-life patterns, problems and relationships that set in motion those of today. If relevant, the patient heals these in forgiveness. He also cuts the psychic cords that may bind him to the past. (This is particularly important when dealing with Karmic ties to our parents.) Finally, the patient integrates and merges with his own past-life personalities. He is then free to use the wisdom of those experiences in his life today.

At the end of a session, which can take three or four hours, (and sometimes longer) I work on the chakras, the etheric meridians and the aura, with crystals. I then seal the aura and say a prayer of thanks.

Fifteen years ago a Jungian analyst friend, Jack, came to me for a session. At the end of it he said: 'What you are doing is a form of "instant" psychoanalysis. I've been trained to take two or three years to get in touch with some of the answers that have come up today. I'm confused and unsure whether this is good or bad. Is there a relapse afterwards?'

I replied that perhaps three hours instead of three years was not suitable for everyone. By the same token, many of the people who came to me had neither the time nor the money for extended psychoanalysis.

Jack returned to his orthodox and analytical practice. Despite his reservations and possible disapproval, I continued my unorthodox and intuitive practice. There is a place for both of us. Today Jack and I occasionally refer patients to each other, if we feel they will benefit. Since then, I have worked with many doctors, psychiatrists, psychoanalysts and psychotherapists. Most of them use past-life therapy as part of their treatment. What was unorthodox has become almost mainstream.

Paracelsus, the 16th century German alchemist, said that a true physician should speak of what was invisible, because all else was knowledge from symptoms which even an untrained person could also recognise. 'He becomes a physician only when he knows that which is unnamed, invisible and immaterial, yet has its effect.'

Past-life or regression therapy makes visible what is unnamed and yet has its effect. I'm sure Paracelsus would approve of the increasing number of therapists who use it today.

6

PERSONAL LIFE HISTORIES

I should like people to share in my belief in reincarnation. I think it would cause them to be much happier, much less frightened, and more sane.

DENYS KELSEY, MB, MRSP

Sixteen years ago, after a lecture on reincarnation at the Festival for Mind, Body and Spirit in London, a woman from the audience asked me: 'If reincarnation is a fact, why can't you prove it?' She added that anyone who claimed a past life must be making it up. 'Either that or it's merely their imagination!' she said scornfully.

I replied that I was unable to 'prove' reincarnations (although others were attempting to do so.) I believed in it but, even if I did not, just to imagine the possibility would change my life. Each movement, meeting, event and relationship would have greater significance. I said: 'The "proof" for me lies in the carthartic relief experienced by most people who choose to undergo regression therapy.'

The response from my inquisitor was: 'Give me some examples. Tell me some stories.'

Here they are.

You will reincarnate whether or not you believe you will. It is much easier if your theories fit reality, but if they do not you will not change the nature of reincarnation one iota.

SETH via JANE ROBERTS, *Seth Material*

The Wounded Heart

Dorothy was an Australian woman in her late sixties. For most of her life she had suffered from cardiac disease. When I met her she was due to go into hospital for open heart surgery. She had never heard of reincarnation, regression, or any other form of alternative therapy.

A mutual friend, worried at Dorothy's increasing panic at the thought of the operation, suggested that she saw me. We arranged an appointment for Friday afternoon. Her operation was scheduled for the following Tuesday. Dorothy appeared to be as apprehensive about her visit to me as she was about going to hospital.

I explained to Dorothy the type of session I did, and asked her to lie down. Two minutes later she bounced up and said: 'I've never done anything like this before, and I don't think I can. Thank you for everything, but I think it's better for both of us if I go.' Secretly I felt the same way, but decided to persevere. I suggested that we at least go into the first part of the session, in which we would examine the details of her present life. I said that if at any time she wanted to stop we would do so, but, 'Why not give it a try?'

Dorothy had never before told her entire life story to another human being. During the course of her relating it we both laughed, shouted and cried together. She lost all trace of self-consciousness, and relaxed completely. 'Dorothy, d'you want to continue?' I asked. 'How could I stop now?' she replied.

I suggested that she concentrate on her heart, not as an organ in her body, but as a symbol for something else. I said: 'Think of the pain you suffer from your heart, and the frustration you feel when you cannot always do what you want. What happened to set this in motion?'

In a flash, and to my amazement, Dorothy became rigid on the bed. Her eyes rolled from side to side. 'What's happening?' I whispered. 'I am the sacrifice. I have been chosen,' Dorothy answered. 'I'm lying on a stone slab and I can see lots of people around me who are chanting. I'm wearing a white robe. The priest gave me a herbal drink, and I'm feeling very disoriented.'

As she described the priest's approach to the stone altar on which she lay, Dorothy's voice changed completely. Initially proud at being the one chosen, and acquiescent to her sacrificial death, Dorothy suddenly saw the bloodlust in the priest's eyes as he plunged the knife into her heart. She died, recognising that what she had believed to be sacred ritual, was in reality an excuse for murder. Her dying thoughts of betrayal, futility and waste brought Dorothy into her present life with a wounded heart – not as a punishment, but in order to heal it.

The re-living of this memory had an almost miraculous effect. When Dorothy went into hospital as planned the surgeon, after many more tests, decided not to operate. Dorothy returned home and, ten years later, continues to enjoy life to the full.

All souls are subject to the trials of reincarnation. They know not how they are being at all times judged, both before coming into this world and when they leave it. They do not know how many

> transformations and mysterial trials they must undergo. The souls must re-enter the absolute substance whence they have emerged. But to accomplish this they must develop all the perfections, the germ of which is planted in them; and if they have not fulfilled this condition during one life they must commence another, a third and so forth.
>
> RABBI SIMEON BEN JOCHAL, *The Zohar*

Of course this does not mean that every person will get the same result. Rosemary, an old and dear friend, had chronic heart problems which finally led to a heart transplant. Over the years Rosemary and I did a lot of things together, including a number of one-to-one sessions. Through these Rosemary got a complete overview of why her life and health were as they were. This did not save her life. A few months after her transplant Rosemary had a relapse and died. However, she did understand what her life purpose had been, and knew that she had achieved it. Rosemary was, and I'm sure still is, brave, funny, witty and wise. Healing in this case was Rosemary's release from her physical body. I'm sure she will be back very soon.

The Wild Woman

William, a quiet, home-loving schoolteacher, came to see me to discuss his marriage. His wife, Tessa, was an ardent feminist. According to William, Tessa was so busy attending meetings to promote Women's Lib that he rarely saw her. Initially supportive of her activities, William felt they now irritated and threatened him. He continued: 'Whenever I try to talk to her about this she accuses me of being a male chauvinist pig, and tells me I am jealous of her new friends; she will fight me tooth and nail if I try to put her down or restrict her.'

William went on to describe his shock when, returning home from school, he walked into his living-room to find a dozen naked women cavorting about in a circle while music played softly in the background. This was now a weekly event. A few days later William came home unexpectedly to collect some papers. He found the same naked women sitting on the floor in rapt silence as they drew one another's vaginas.

'I appreciate modern women's fight for equality,' said William, 'but what has all this got to do with it?'

I suggested to William that he read Esther Harding's book *Women's Mysteries, Ancient and Modern* in which she says: 'The woman in this culture is cut off from the springs of life in the depths of her own being.' It could perhaps be that for Tessa and her friends to dance naked, and even to draw one another's vaginas, as an instinctive attempt to re-connect to these same springs of life.

Dancing induces ecstasy. Ecstasy – or ek-stasis – means to be outside oneself, to move beyond one's logical and conditioned mind. In the past women shamans and seers danced, usually in groups of twelve, to anchor spiritual energy and generate fertility into the earth. They were revered as keepers of the Mysteries, oracles who, through their dance, bridged between heaven and earth, and kept cosmic forces in balance.

I reminded William that many women in the early 1900s grew up ashamed of their bodies, sexuality and creativity. Much of this was inherited from ancient patriarchal suppression.

'To be fully developed as a human being is to be born a male,' said Saint Thomas Aquinas. 'Among all savage beasts none is found so harmful as a woman,' said Saint John Chrysostom. 'What a misfortune to be a woman!'

remarked Soren Kierkegaard. 'Woman in her greatest perfection was made to serve and obey man,' added John Knox.

The recent Victorian era in which even table-legs were considered to be fraught with sexual innuendo has not helped. I quote a psychiatrist who said that to be a successful wife, mother and housewife today (i.e. nearly 20 years ago) a woman almost needed a lobectomy (removal of a lobe of the brain). The traditional demands upon woman were such a denial of her individuality and creativity that hundreds and thousands rebelled against it.

Tessa's plunge into feminist activity was part of her role in this rebellion, as well as her attempt to re-connect herself to her own primeval femaleness.

When William met Tessa he thought he had found his ideal woman. She appeared to have all the attributes of a perfect wife. Now, confused by her transition from goddess to apparent witch/bitch, William was afraid that the heterosexual woman he had married had turned into a rampant lesbian. 'Neither of us is happy. We blame each other for our problems. Maybe the best thing for both of us is to split up,' said William at the end of our conversation.

Two days later Tessa appeared on my doorstep. 'Why am I so deeply concerned with Women's Lib? Where did it start?' she asked me.

Tessa's regression initially took her back to the memory of a female life in Calcutta. She was the ruler's sister but, despite his power and the family's wealth, Tessa lived the life of an oppressed Indian woman. She was never allowed out alone, and must always wear a veil.

One day, bored and rebellious, Tessa bribed her maid to take her down to the docks. Amidst the hustle and bustle of boats arriving, departing and unloading, Tessa, feeling anonymous among the crowds, lowered her veil. As she did so she caught the eye of an Englishman descending the gangplank of his newly-arrived ship. This man, thinking that Tessa's gesture was deliberately flirtatious, followed her home. His subsequent meeting with Tessa's brother and family impelled him to ask for her hand in marriage. This was refused.

The Englishman was sent away. Tessa, now considered to be a source of shame to her family, was killed by her brother.

Tessa's 'crime' was to be born female in a culture where women were penalised for being women. (I am not an ardent feminist, but I do find it very strange that throughout history so many men have denied a woman's value when, without women, they would not have been born in the first place.)

Tessa later regressed into memories of sexual abuse, both as a Roman slave girl, and as a London prostitute who sold her favours to provide food for her children. In these, and in other lives, Tessa began to resist male power and domination. Towards the end of the session she suddenly said that she was a 'wild woman'.

In fact, in ancient times 'wild women' from many cultures were in reality priestesses who worshipped the Great Mother. They held the responsibility for the continuation of human life. Full of joy (sometimes induced by drugs or 'magic' mushrooms) they danced, sang, and performed rites in caves or on mountain-tops to attune to the spirit of life embodied within the Earth itself. Men were not allowed to join in. The women sometimes even killed them if they inadvertently crossed the threshold.

When the patriarchy took over, it generally banned women's rites. Today, men and women are becoming equal, and even androgynous (a combination of male and female). Many women feel intuitively and strongly the need to go back to some of the ancient rites in order to re-charge their femininity or female power. Many men fear the same power.

Tessa now saw that her strong commitment to the Women's Movement stemmed from many lives of abuse and oppression. She also recognised that William had been the Englishman in Calcutta who, unaware of Indian social customs regarding women at that time, had unintentionally caused her death. He also played a role in some of her other past lives. Tessa realised that her defiant attitude to William when she danced was her unconscious way of saying: 'You are *not* going to be the death of me this time!'

Tessa continued to fight for women's rights, but without her former aggression. William's and Tessa's new clarity about their past relationships saved their marriage.

The Wise Woman

My next brush with past-life matriarchy was at Los Angeles airport. En route between Sydney and London I had a three-hour stopover. Because this did not allow enough time for me to visit the city, a friend came to keep me company at the airport. Our initial greeting over, Francesca surprised me by saying: 'Could you do a session with me here – not a full session, but enough for me to find out where you and I knew each other before?'

Surrounded as we were by the bustle of people, baggage carts, irritable children and crying babies, I doubted that such a session was possible. We finally decided to give it a try. There was nowhere to sit, so we found a corner on the floor, where we could lean against the wall and stretch our legs out. Almost immediately Francesca began to describe a life as a female scientist/astronomer in an ancient matri-archal society. She appeared to wield enormous power.

Francesca saw herself studying the heavens, the movements of planets and stars within the solar system. She was surrounded by a mass of intricate equipment including strange glittering instruments and powerful telescopes.

The women she ruled used psychic means – telepathy, clairvoyance, teleportation and prophesy – to accomplish most of their work. Francesca saw them erect huge buildings and standing stones from mind power alone. The men, though not badly treated, were subservient to the women, and obediently carried out their orders. Francesca then described ceremonies in which she sat under an immense dome (similar to a giant hairdryer) and channelled information to the community. One of the messages said that the time for a matriarchal society was over. The women must now step down and share their wisdom and power with the men. They refused to do this. The result was that the Hierarchy (the spiritual guardians of the universe) stepped in and offered beings from other planets the opportunity to incarnate on the earth.

These star people, though born in the normal way, were very different from human babies. Suddenly Francesca gasped and said: 'You were there too! You were chosen to separate out human and non-human babies at birth. All those who appeared to be not of the earth were immediately destroyed.' My stomach churned. Although I myself had never seen, let alone sensed, the life she described, I felt that what she said was true.

Tears rolled down Francesca's cheeks. 'I had the authority to stop this, I chose not to. I turned a blind eye and shut myself away with my science and astronomy.' She then said: 'I can see that you became sickened by the murder of the babies, and you began to pass them all through as humans. Those who were particularly deformed or different you smuggled away and brought up yourself. Your actions were later discovered, and you were put to death for treason. As the star children grew up, they rebelled against the matriarchy, and it gradually collapsed.'

When Francesca opened her eyes, she went on to say: 'Now I know, not only where I met you, but also why I am so strongly opposed to abortion, and believe in promoting life at all costs.'

We were both exhausted by Francesca's revelations. The release of strongly repressed emotional energy can leave one feeling drained and empty, but also healed. I caught my onward plane to London with a great sense of lightness and freedom.

Years later I described Francesca's session to an American psychic I met at a conference. I said: 'Obviously the decline of the matriarchy came about for many reasons, but do you think that Francesca's story of the Hierarchy introducing star people into the earth plane has an element of truth to it?'

The psychic was so shocked that she had to sit down. 'As you spoke,' she said, 'I had a sudden revelation that, not only was I one of the original star people on earth, but also that I was one of the babies saved and brought up by you.'

Forced To Fit

Sheer weight brought Margaret to see me. She weighed 18 stone. Most of her present life problems were the result of the despair and self-hatred induced by her size. Despite numerous and varied diets the fat remained. I found it interesting that when Margaret described her family, her school, or her work, she constantly used phrases such as 'I don't fit in. I didn't fit in. I cannot fit in.' (I mention this

because research in America has shown a direct corre-
lation between the language we use and our physical
health.)

When Margaret regressed to the memory of another life
she said she was a Spanish señorita, the spoiled only
daughter of a wealthy Sevillian family. From her
childhood her parents spared no effort or expense to
prepare her for her introduction into the best of Sevillian
society. Almost as soon as Margaret was born her mother
made ambitious plans for a brilliant marriage for her
daughter.

In Spain at this time – about 150 years ago – it was
fashionable for a young woman to have a tiny waist, one
that would entice a prospective husband to think
longingly of clasping it in his two hands. To achieve such
a waist, Margaret was encased every day in a corset which
her maid pulled tight. Margaret loathed it and said to her
mother: 'If this is what I have to endure to get a husband
I would rather not get married!' Her mother ignored her,
and told Margaret's maid to tighten the corset a little
more every day. When Margaret was 18 the maid pulled
the corset so tight that Margaret's lungs were crushed and
she died. Her dying thought was: 'I'll never be held in
again. I don't care if I don't fit what the rest of the society
thinks is proper!'

Margaret was astonished when these words popped out
of her own mouth, and then she began to laugh until she
almost wept. She now understood the reason for her size,
and left my flat still laughing. A few months later I
bumped into Margaret in the street. I hardly recognised
her. While still no Twiggy she was a very reduced version
of the Margaret I had first met. 'How did you do it?' I
asked, thinking that I would use the same diet. 'I haven't
done anything,' she replied. 'The weight simply began to
fall off by itself after I'd seen myself in that Spanish life.'

Allergic To The Past

Jenny, even as a tiny girl, had a very stormy relationship with her mother. Now a woman in her thirties and happily married, she was exhausted from her constant battles with her mother, now widowed, who was always descending on them and trying to interface in their relationship. Jenny told me that her aversion to her mother was so great that even as a newly-born baby she became allergic to her mother's milk. This led to an allergy to all dairy products.

During our investigation, Jenny discovered that, in another life in the 1880s, she and her mother had been sisters in competition for the same man. After much skulduggery, the sister (now the mother) won, and married the man. Jenny became an embittered spinster and, unfulfilled, always blamed her sister for it. Once Jenny recognised the source of her festering resentment towards her mother, she was able to release it from her present life. This healed their relationship, and her allergies gradually disappeared.

Tom was another allergy-sufferer. He gained 80 per cent relief after past-life therapy. From his childhood Tom's life (and that of his family) had been made miserable by not just one, but numerous food allergies. During his regression, Tom saw himself as an alcoholic and a glutton. Despite his then family's pleas to pull himself together, Tom ignored them and ate and drank his way to an early grave. His body in *this* life would not allow him to do the same thing again, and he was forced to pay constant attention to it. Tom and I worked together two or three times, and gradually many, though not all, of his allergies faded away.

Regression therapy has successfully treated a wide range of physical ailments. Many people whose lives were almost untenable due to particular phobias (an illogical, deep-seated fear) or chronic depression seemed to experience a genuine improvement when confronted by the apparent source of their problems.

Dr Raymond Moody says: 'It should not be a surprise that people note improvements in their physical condition after undergoing successful regression experiences. After all, it is not uncommon for patients in regular psychotherapy to overcome physical illness after extended therapy. With regressions, the mental problems causing an illness are often tapped much more quickly, as the past-life experiences go to the heart of the emotion.'

A Way Of Healing

Past-life therapy recognises the interrelatedness between mind, feelings, body and spirit. In a sense, it is a form of psychosomatic healing. Originally doctors ridiculed the idea that the mind and emotions could create illness in the body. Today's research shows that there is indeed often a link.

In his book *Life Before Life*, Dr Raymond Moody quotes Irene Hickman, editor of the American Journal of Regression Therapy, who said: 'The Members of the Association for Past-Life Research use techniques that uncover and reveal happenings from the past – sometimes long distant past – which are causing present illness, disharmony or malfunction. We have found within our own experience that when a patient or client has a problem of any kind, there is a cause, that this cause can be elicited using regression techniques, that the cause can be so treated as to neutralise the effect, allowing a return to health.'

Towards the end of her article Irene Hickman also

wrote: 'We are convinced that we have found, and are continuing to find, answers that are important to the family of man. We will enhance understanding, enable the development of greater health, harmony, inner peace and creativity. The techniques we use are helping our patients/clients to reach their optimum creativity.'

When Irene Hickman wrote this article in 1986 most of the members of The Association for Past-Life Research used hypnotism to induce past-life recall. Hypnotism bypasses the present-day personality, whereas deep relaxation allows simultaneous contact with both present and past personalities. In the 1990s many therapists obtain the same results from deep relaxation and light trance.

What I enjoy about my own technique (which evolved as I described earlier) is that my patient, though relaxed, is always fully aware and in control. He may have his eyes open or closed, get up, walk about or stretch, go to the bathroom or sip water, without affecting his living of whatever memories may come up. In fact one man, halfway through the session, remembered that he should put more money in the parking meter. He jumped out of an Arabian life, in which he was a wealthy trader leading a string of camels across the desert, and returned five minutes later to see himself further on in the same life choosing new women for his harem.

I am there to help, but my patient/client has to do the work himself. This is what can catalyse major change. Whatever takes place comes out of the psyche of the individual, and not because I say: 'Do this!' or 'Do that!'

Two Readings

Although I am sometimes asked to give readings I usually refuse. I developed an allergic reaction to this type of work after I saw Paul Solomon and others submerged by similar requests. Most of these requests were from people who refused to take responsibility for their own lives, and wanted to be told exactly what to do. I prefer to work with people who want to link into their own inner wisdom, and from that make their own decisions.

An exception to this was Florence, usually known as Flo. I did a reading for her spontaneously. Flo was a tiny black-skinned African woman, born and brought up in a mud hut in Kenya. By the time she was sixteen Flo was the mother of two illegitimate daughters, begotten by different men who had subsequently disappeared. Friends of mine, the MacNamaras, employed her to help their gardener. Virtually uneducated, Flo was set to work to sweep leaves and weed flowerbeds.

When the MacNamaras realised that Flo was quick-witted and hard-working they decided to take her into their house and teach her how to cook and sew. Flo's cooking, to the relief of Mobutu, the MacNamaras' long-term cook, was a disaster. He suggested that the family should encourage Flo's apparent aptitude for sewing and keep her out of the kitchen.

Flo became so proficient at mending, embroidery, and even knitting, that she developed a clientele amongst the MacNamaras' friends.

I happened to be visiting Kenya and the MacNamaras for six weeks, to give lectures and seminars, when Flo stumbled into my life. Apparently Mobutu told Flo: 'There's a white *mganga* (witchdoctor) in the house. Many women come to see her. Perhaps you should see her too.' With the MacNamaras' permission, she did so, though we inevitably had problems – she spoke only pidgin English, and I no Kiswahili. Her biggest preoccupation, bringing up two daughters now in their teens and with no man's help, was that she had never had a present in her life, whereas all her women friends had had many gifts. This lack of a present seemed far more of a blight on her life than all her sufferings through extreme poverty.

As we talked, I saw this scenario flowing out from the left side of her head: she was a dazzlingly beautiful Ethiopian courtesan with fine features and a light brown skin, swathed in richly-coloured silks, carried everywhere on a litter, surrounded by handmaidens. She never put a foot to the ground. Even to bathe, she was lowered into the turquoise waters of a shallow pool where waiting women washed, massaged, and oiled her. Reclined on her cushions again, she greeted the many men who came to her, vying for her favours with their magnificent gifts ranging from egg-sized rubies and emeralds to amethysts from the coral depths of the Red Sea.

It is not for the first time that you live garbed in
   this human form;
Again you will be born, again you will meet death.
With each passing period becoming more
   enlightened.
Finally because of these transitions,
You will attain the ultimate perfection of human
   nature;
Now, as a nature soul you will rise high above us
   all,
Suddenly as a new star appears among the stars in
   rank with gods.

APOLLON N. MAYKOV, *Album of Antinay*

I asked her if her religion included the belief in past lives. 'No,' she replied, 'I'm a Catholic.' I then told her in simple terms what I had seen. The idea of her having had such an exotic life delighted her, and her whole face lit up. I explained to her that it was because she had then lived entirely from men and their presents that she had had none in her life today. So overjoyed was she by this discovery that with sparkling eyes and a beaming smile she ran off to the kitchen to tell Mobutu. I followed, and reminded her that with her sewing skills she was now independent in a way in which most of her women friends were not. There was now nothing to stop her choosing her own present (or man) as she wanted.

In each of the years that followed when I revisited Kenya, I found that Flo's new and positive attitude to life had lasted and blossomed.

Another spontaneous reading which really helped a life was one Paul Solomon did for Sophula Leontidi.

Sophula was the daughter of an extremely wealthy Greek shipping family. After attending one of Paul's seminars in London, Sophula invited both Paul and myself to Greece to inaugurate a centre for arts, music and philosophy that she had built on the coast, about an hour's drive from Athens. She suggested that, instead of staying in a hotel in Athens, it would be more convenient for her, and much more fun for us, if we spent ten days as her guests on the boat she kept moored near the centre.

Expecting some kind of yacht or cabin-cruiser, I was astounded when the boat turned out to be an enormous vessel built on the lines of an ocean-going liner. As we mounted the gangplank, rows of what looked like half the Greek navy greeted us. They were in reality Sophula's staff.

After settling us on board, Sophula said: 'We'll now take the motor-boat and I'll show you the centre from the sea. We'll visit it properly tomorrow.'

Twenty minutes later, she pointed to an immense building perched on the cliffs above us. I saw a blend of palace and temple bathed pink by the setting sun. It struck me speechless with awe. In my imagination it seemed a great brooding stone lion crouching in anticipation of a touch from a Greek god or goddess to bring it alive.

When Sophula greeted us next morning, she was clad in two turquoise bath-towels, one round her breasts, the other round her hips. She had secured each towel with a gold safety-pin, from which hung the Greek symbol of protection against evil or bad luck – a large blue (sometimes turquoise) eye. During our entire stay, the only time I saw Sophula out of her towels and into a dress was when Paul gave his weekend inaugural seminar.

After breakfast we piled into the motorboat and set off for our second view of the centre, this time from the inside. To this day it remains for me one of the most stunning and beautiful buildings I have ever seen. We wandered through a maze of arches, pillars and court-yards, many of which were built around ancient olive trees. We dabbled our toes in sunken indoor pools as big as tennis-courts, filled with aquamarine water which cast rippling shadows on the walls.

On the roof Paul, Sophula and myself sat on stone seats carefully placed in the shade of trees laden with lemons and apricots. As we gazed out across seemingly endless azure skies, Sophula said abruptly: 'Paul, I must talk to you. I'm having a very difficult time with my family. They are extremely worried about the money I've spent and continue to spend on this place. My brothers think I've gone crazy, and have threatened to take legal action to stop me using my share of the family money in this way. They cannot understand that this building, and the spiritual teachings I hope will take place within it, are the fulfilment of dreams I've had since my childhood. Every country except Greece seems to have easy access to the wave of new visions and ideas that now sweep the world. I want this centre to provide similar opportunities for my fellow Greeks, but my family may stop me.'

Paul gestured her to stop. 'I see you in another life,' he said, 'born in Jerusalem some fifty years after the crucifixion. You hear about the life and death of Jesus, and are very upset to learn that Jesus was born in a stable. You tell many people that if you had been alive at the time you would have ensured that he was born in a palace.'

Paul then described some of Sophula's past lives, in most of which she was very poor. She always kept a deep love of God in her heart. Sophula had two or three lives tending the gardens around the Mystery Schools or Temples of Wisdom in Ancient Egypt. She yearned to be a student, but could only watch what went on from afar. These lives stimulated her deep desire to acquire spiritual knowledge.

'Your commitment to Jesus has never wavered,' Paul went on. 'Hence you have this glorious opportunity to study spiritual truths yourself, and to provide a fine way for others to do so too.'

This so heartened Sophula that she stood firm for her rights and beliefs, and her family finally accepted them.

Fear Of Loving

While Sophula had yearned to enter a temple, Pamela's past experience in one proved fatal. Pamela was so sexually inhibited that she could not bear her husband to touch her. In Pamela's session she saw herself as a priestess in a temple in which sex was used as part of a ritual. At first she was trained in a form of tantric yoga in which there was no physical touch. A priest and priestess faced each other and mentally raised their energies from the root or base chakra to the crown. When they were proficient at this, they were taught how to blend their crown chakra energies with each other.

Pamela then described another level of sexual training. In a very circumscribed setting and ritualistic manner, the priest and priestess were brought together for the purpose of full sexual contact. Teachers carefully monitored it, and seconds before orgasm interrupted and pulled them apart. This practice was repeated again and again, day after day. Finally the frustration caused by their never completing the sexual act created a powerful telepathic link between the priest and priestess. This telepathy was later used during intricate occult rites within the temple.

The sexual relationship between a priest and priestess was meant to be impersonal – an aspect of their esoteric training. Even though it was forbidden, priests and priestesses sometimes fell in love with one another. This is what happened to Pamela and her priest. Unable to confine their sexual relationship within the limits imposed on them, they met secretly and were subsequently discovered. Pamela's priest-lover was cast out of the temple, while she herself was put to death.

Pamela realised that in this life she embodied the fear that to give all of herself, in love or sex, would lead to disaster. In a later session with Pamela's husband, Tony, he recognised that he had been the cast-out priest from that same past life. Pamela's subconscious recognition of him had triggered even greater sexual frigidity than might have occurred with another man. Again, the understanding that Pamela and Tony both gained from remembering these experiences healed her of her sexual inhibitions.

Jane had no fear of sex, but a terror of pregnancy. She was also reluctant to have a session with me 'for fear of what might be revealed,' she said. So Jane and I simply talked over a cup of coffee at her kitchen table. She had been married for ten years to David. They both felt that if they did not produce children soon they never would. Jane was torn between her desire to provide David with the family he wanted, and the black despair that overwhelmed her when she thought of pregnancy and the act of birth itself.

Seven years earlier, Jane had imagined that she was pregnant. It had turned out to be a false alarm, but she had freaked out so badly that she had ended up in hospital with a complete nervous breakdown. David thought that Jane's present qualms stemmed from this breakdown. Jane believed that her terror of childbirth had caused it in the first place.

When I suggested that Jane's panic might come from another life she ridiculed the idea. I then remembered a number of sessions in which a person's cellular memory of a catastrophe was passed on into the bodies of his descendants. This genetic memory acted as an unconscious trigger for the person carrying the memory imprint to go through a similar trauma at exactly the same age.

For example, I'm twenty and engaged to be married. Two days before the wedding my fiancé is killed in a car accident. I am devastated, so much so that I become ill and almost die. Fifteen years later I meet and marry another man and subsequently have a child. My child at precisely twenty experiences a major life-changing and similar trauma. This imprint can also be passed on to his children and even grandchildren.

As I spoke, Jane interrupted me, crying: 'That's it! That's me! Until you described this type of cellular or genetic memory, I had completely forgotten. My great-grandmother died giving birth to my grandmother, May. My grandmother died when she gave birth to my mother. My mother was brought up by her aunts who, even when she was small, used to say to her: "If it wasn't for you, May would still be alive. You caused May's death!" My mother in turn had a very difficult time when I was born, though she did not tell me this till I was sixteen when I also learned how she had been blamed for her own mother's death. I'm sure that I must have inherited her fear that birth causes death.'

It was a great relief to her that there was a possible rational reason for her terror, and that it was not the onset of madness. It reduced Jane to tears. About five years later she gave birth to a daughter, Polly. Hopefully, Polly will not embody the same trauma, but if she does Jane will know how to help her.

Of course you don't die, nobody dies, death doesn't exist, you only reach a new level of vision, a new realm of consciousness, a new unknown world. Just as you don't know where you came from, so you don't know where you're going. But there is something there, before and after, I firmly believe.

HENRY MILLER

The Case Against Fantasy

Quite recently I read that strongly visual people can easily fantasise other lives – just as an author can write stories about people he has never met. The article continued: 'These fantasies simply compensate for the boredom of their (owners') present existence.'

I am sure that in some cases this may be true, but in my experience most past-life memories are fairly ordinary, and merely mirror unresolved situations from this present life. Also, if past-life memory is pure fantasy, why do so many people gain such life-changing benefits from it – especially when many do not believe in reincarnation in the first place?

For example, during a visit to a women's prison I met Meg and Lily. Meg, at 20, was serving life imprisonment for the murder of her husband. She had married at 17, and her husband had constantly beaten her up. This she had stood, but not when he began abusing their baby daughter too. She killed him in the baby's defence. Lily was 'in' for from eight to ten years (dependent on good behaviour). The police had picked her up for speeding, and then allegedly found a dozen bags of heroin in the back seat of her car. She swore that this was a plant, and her story sounded credible.

Both women asked me for a private consultation. The prison governor agreed, but stipulated that each could only have ten minutes. I suggested to Meg and Lily that I should see them together, so extending our time to 20 minutes. They agreed. Though neither had ever even heard of reincarnation, I put them through a quick regression. Both gained instant insight into the past-life background of why they were in prison today. Meg saw herself as having been murdered most cruelly by the man who was her husband in her present life. Lily's past-life vision was of herself as an army officer ruthlessly imprisoning enemy prisoners.

We had not time to discuss these insights any more profoundly, for warders marched them back promptly to their cells. But eight months later both Meg and Lily were released. It was as if, having linked in to the root cause of their present imprisonment, their recognition released the Karmic need for them to be in prison any longer. Although I saw other prisoners privately, Meg and Lily were the only two I regressed. No other prisoner was released.

Becky was 29. She had never been out of Australia in her life, and was so young that she knew virtually nothing about World War II. Her greatest concern was her beloved three-year-old daughter. She was brave enough to volunteer to take part in a session with me which ABC Television wanted to film in my motel room.

The camera crew of five tough Australians pitched up like a gang of navvies, in shirtsleeves, smoking continually and obviously highly sceptical of the mere idea of reincarnation. I myself was doubtful about the success of the venture, due to their attitude, to the excessively bright lighting, and to the two or three cameras constantly focused on our every move. The programme interviewer, a girl, was more sympathetic and encouraging.

I told Becky to lie down, close her eyes and breathe deeply to help her relax. We talked a little of her pending divorce. I asked her to look back and see if she could find a cause for it, however remote.

She screamed suddenly, and panted, gasped and grunted like someone chased by the hounds of hell. Her whole body contorted as if she carried a precious bundle close to her chest. She kept looking in desperation over her shoulder. The whimpers and horrendous sounds that came from her made the hairs on my arms and the back of my neck stand on end. The formerly mocking camera crew were shocked rigid, and the interviewer had to remind them to keep the cameras rolling.

Becky then described hiding in a cellar, into which she had crawled on her hands and knees, nursing her precious bundle in front of her. But soldiers found her quickly, and marched her off to a station, where a long line of cattle-trucks waited. The soldiers wrenched from her the baby she was carrying, and flung it up and away like a sack of rags. It bounced on the roof of a cattle-truck and disappeared over the other side. She was never to see it again.

The guards then pushed her into a cattle-truck, so crowded that there was barely room to stand. The journey lasted for hours. There was little air and no water. For much of the night they were shunted onto a siding. At their final destination, shouting guards forced them all out. They stood bewildered, blinking in the light. The soldiers marched them off to a long, flat-roofed building where they ordered them to take off all their clothes (which in theory were to be fumigated and returned to them). They also shaved their heads (again supposedly for hygienic reasons). Then all of them, men, women and children, were ushered naked into the so-called shower buildings from which they would never return. The showers would pour forth, not water, but fatal Zyklon B gas.

After she had finished her narrative, Becky sobbed her heart out. I held and rocked her. The interviewer asked her if she had ever experienced anything like this before. No, she answered. How did she think that this experience had benefited her? Becky replied that she felt lighter and relieved on a certain level. 'Even my body feels different!' she said. The interviewer agreed: 'Even your eyes and skin look different!' Becky added, 'Now I know where my fear of losing my daughter came from, I shall stop being so possessive of her, and allow her more freedom.'

Everyone in the room felt as though they had been through this Nazi terror with Becky. The camera crew in particular left in a very chastened mood.

I believe that these stories are significant evidence of reincarnation. But who knows? Does it really matter? What mattered is that each person gained new insight, self-understanding and a deep inner peace that enabled them to make profound changes in his life. Edgar Allen Poe put it neatly:

It is mere idleness to say I had not lived before – that

*the soul has no previous existence . . . You deny it? –
Let us not argue the matter. Convinced myself, I seek
not to convince.*

7

WHO OR WHAT
INCARNATES?

*In the beginning God created the heaven and the
earth...*
*And God said: Let us make man in our own image,
after our likeness ...*
*So God created man in his own image, in the image
of God created He him, male and female created
He them.*

GENESIS, 1:1, 26, 27

During a visit to America in 1979 I was unexpectedly
invited to give a seminar on male–female relationships. As
I had married the first man who asked me because a) I
was far too young to know any better, and b) I had always
been told I was so awful that no man would ever marry
me – which resulted in a painfully difficult marriage and
subsequent divorce – I did not feel that I was the best
person to give such a seminar. However, the original
leader was ill, so I agreed.

I had 24 hours in which to prepare myself. I spent 12 of
them frantically trying to think of questions to ask my
seminar group, questions that would stimulate in them an
awareness of how balanced (or not) they were with their
own feminine and masculine qualities. For example,

whether male or female, are you the one who always makes the decisions at home or at work, or the one who meekly follows what others tell you to do?

Masculine energy is assertive, active and outgoing. Feminine energy is receptive, imaginative, intuitive and inward-looking. We need to balance both – sometimes I talk, sometimes I listen – sometimes I dig the garden or scrub the kitchen floor (masc.) and sometimes I loll in a fragrant bath or in front of a roaring fire (fem.). Most of our imbalance comes from our parental relationships. Our mothers and fathers (although we chose them) are the role models for whether we accept or reject our own male and female attributes.

Thus, the dynamics of our parents' relationship to each other is usually mirrored back to us. Unconsciously, they offload onto us the unresolved conflicts between them. This in turn affects our own attitude to ourselves and others. However, instead of blaming a mother or father we should ask ourselves: 'Why was I born into that family? What am I meant to learn from this man and woman?'

Our parents also mirror what we ourselves have been in the past. Part of our life purpose is to synthesise what our parents represent to us, and take it to another level. For example, my father is a happy-go-lucky gambler, and my mother a regular churchgoer and member of the Women's Institute. I look at what each represents to me: perhaps my mother symbolises responsibility, duty, obligation to others and selflessness, whereas my father is a combination of joy, laughter, irresponsibility and selfishness. (I'm sure not all churchgoing Women's Institute members are joyless!) I must therefore now see how I can blend responsibility with joy of life, bring together joy in worship, take life less seriously, with a light heart.

This is the kind of realisation that I now hoped to get

across to my audience. I then at last went to bed and slept.

Two hours later, as if hands grabbed my shoulders and shook me, I awoke with a start. The room seemed to pulse with an invisible but electrifying energy. A voice in my ear said: 'Everything you have done today is from a logical psycho-analytic point of view – now look at this!'

As if at the movies, I saw unfolding before me scenes of incredible beauty – mountains, hills, lakes and valleys, rivers, streams and tumbling waterfalls filled my vision. Animals of every kind appeared to cavort and gather together in perfect harmony.

I then saw semi-invisible creatures in the form of man, but without a solid physical body. I thought I was being shown spiritual beings, the sons and daughters of God (although they were androgynous) or souls when they came to earth for the first time. For them the earth was like a wonderful garden in which to play and explore.

Fascinated by their discoveries, they began to project themselves into trees, rocks, flowers and animals to experience what it felt like. While many came and went as they pleased, others identified so completely with whatever they were projected into that they forgot their true spiritual nature and became stuck. A new wave of souls then came to earth to help release those who were imprisoned. Using colour, music, sound and touch, they tried to re-awaken their lost spiritual brothers and sisters and remind them of their divine origins. (Most alternative methods of healing attempt to do exactly the same thing.) These souls were so intrigued by how animals procreated that they decided to copy them. Some did this out of pure curiosity, others as a means of communicating with the spiritual beings trapped within the animals' bodies. They too became trapped and gradually lost their abilities to project consciousness in and out of matter.

As wave upon wave of rescuing souls came to the earth,

their bodies appeared to become more dense. When they in turn co-habited with animals, they were not only entrapped but also produced offspring that were a mixture of animal and human. I saw creatures with feathers, fur, claws and cloven feet and tails. (Some of them resembled the half-human half-animal creatures such as centaurs, mermaids and birdmen described in various myths and legends that have been handed down to us as pure fantasy.)

I now saw what I can only describe as another level of evolution (spiritual rather than physical). Androgynous souls projected a part of their consciousness out and away from themselves. They literally seemed to split in half and separate the negative or feminine principle from the positive or masculine. This split is what stimulates in so many of us today the deep yearning to find what some call our soul-mate, or twin soul, and which is in reality the other half of ourselves. (Because the soul, no matter whether currently using a male or female body, is feminine to God, this need also triggers our search for God.)

Creation – A New Perspective

Whether or not what I was shown was metaphorical, allegorical or pure spiritual truth, it filled me with excitement and gave me new ideas for my seminar.

I was also forced to re-evaluate my thoughts on creation and evolution. I finally concluded that what I had seen was a mixture of both. Evolving matter may begin in a small way, like algae forming on a pool which then become an amoeba whose structure increases in complexity to become something bigger and better in the form of a fish or frog – and so on and on and on. Evolving souls seemed to be of a different stream of consciousness, which contained within themselves the ability to merge with any and every form of physical matter – from the tiniest ant or blade of grass to the biggest lion, mountain, tree or elephant.

To me it seemed that, if previously created souls could merge with or project themselves into evolving matter, creation and evolution were part and parcel of the same process.

Despite my convent school scripture readings from Genesis, in which we are told that 'God formed man of the dust of the ground and breathed into his nostrils the breath of life, and man became a living soul', I always believed that souls were sparks of light, separate from but connected to the body of God, which I imagined to be as some vast ball of fire and light – a bit like a setting sun. In fact, as a child I talked to the sun as if it were God. I used to look into the sky as the first scattering of stars began to appear, and imagine these were souls cavorting about in heaven. I wondered if they ever fell out of the sky and secretly longed to find a fallen soul/star at my feet, although I knew I would have to hide it from the nuns.

I also found it hard to accept that Eve was made from one of Adam's ribs. However, when I was shown the scenes I have just described, I thought it could have been one interpretation of how androgynous souls divided into male and female.

In his book *Genesis Revisited*, Zecharia Sitchin says that both orientalists and Bible scholars now know that the Book of Genesis is based on ancient Sumerian texts.

In these texts (the Atra Hasis), Sitchin says, are descriptions of how 'rank and file astronauts' were sent to Earth to mine for gold. The work was so backbreaking that the Anunnaki as they were called, finally mutinied. Their leaders wondered if there was another way to extract the gold, and decided to create a primitive worker, or Adamu (meaning earthling) to help. They saw the creature they needed was already there – I suppose a form of apeman – but how to stimulate its intelligence enough to use tools and carry out orders? The texts say: 'Bind upon it the image of the gods.' It appears they did this by a form of genetic manipulation, and so brought an intelligent man into being.

Looking at matter from the most rigidly scientific point of view, the assumption that, amidst the myriad of worlds scattered through endless space, there can be no intelligence, as much greater than man's as his is greater than the blackbeetle's, no being endowed with powers of influencing the course of nature as much greater than his as his is greater than the snail's, seems to me not merely baseless, but impertinent.

THOMAS HENRY HUXLEY

In *Indaba, My Children*, Credo Vusamazulu Mutwa, a Zulu medicine-man and spiritual teacher, says that Zulu legends describe how ancient gold mines were worked by 'artificially produced flesh and blood slaves created by the First People'.

Sitchin says that the Anunnaki (those who came from heaven to earth) arrived about 445,000 years ago, and returned repeatedly. They were facing ecological deterioration that made life on their planet increasingly difficult. They discovered that gold particles suspended as a shield protected their dwindling atmosphere. (Apparently the windows on American spacecraft are coated with a thin layer of gold to shield the astronauts against radiation.)

Sitchin says that, from writings and drawings on Sumerian tablets, it looks as if the original 'Adamu' was the first test-tube baby – a mix of an apewoman's egg fertilised by seeds from the Anunnaki, or 'gods from heaven'. His book suggests that evolution took us to a certain point, and then the gods stepped in to upgrade our level of intelligence and ability. Maybe this is what the Bible meant when it says: 'The sons of God came into the daughters of men, and they bore children to them.'

The word Anunnaki was translated into the Hebrew 'Elohim', which was then accepted as a name for God, whereas in the original Hebrew it meant *gods*. Sitchin's book says that 'Adam' was not a specific person, but one of many 'Adamu' created to be worker-servants, but who were eventually transformed when the gods decided to share much of their knowledge (except the secret of their longevity!) with them. The Sumerian texts describe this as wisdom lowered from heaven, and also suggest that the Anunnakis' first experiments resulted in sterility between the Adamu and his female counterpart. To offset this, further genetic manipulation was done, including a possible bone-marrow transplant in order to stimulate the immune system. This is perhaps where the story of how Eve was created from Adam's rib (or bones) came from.

Sitchin also writes in his book that in 1987 the Dean of Anthropology at the University of Florence in Italy caused a furore when he said that ongoing genetic experiments could lead to the 'creation of a new breed of slave, an anthropoid, with a chimpanzee mother and a human father'. It seems that modern science is simply rediscovering techniques the Sumerians used millions of years ago.

The Sumerian texts described the Anunnaki as gods or astronauts who travelled with ease between other planets and earth. Ruth Montgomery, in her book *The World Before*, also describes repeated visits to earth by spacemen and extra-terrestrials. This means that, long before life began on earth, incredibly advanced civilisations evolved on other planets and planes, and no doubt continue to do so today. To me this suggests that the history of evolution on the earth plane is a tiny, and fairly recent, drop in the ocean, compared to the history of the rest of the cosmos.

Around the world, numerous myths and legends describe how human beings were 'seeded from the stars' to create an individual who was a perfect blend of spirit and matter. If matter gradually evolved when life on earth began, and spirit was brought by gods from outer space, where did this spirit come from in the first place?

As a child I had never heard of the Big Bang theory, but I always sensed that I had been part of something which, like a firework on Guy Fawkes night, suddenly exploded into billions of sparks of light or stars. To me this 'something' was a force, an energy, an intelligence, that I called God. It separated and divided itself up into tiny fragments – rather as I later saw the souls or etheric forms of life divide themselves in half in my vision – only a billion times more abundantly.

Soul And Spirit

At school the nuns referred to the soul and spirit as if they were one and the same thing. I thought then, and still do today, that spirit and soul are different. Of course, I could not then explain why I thought this. Today my understanding is that spirit is the original spark of light that comes from God, soul is the sum total of mind, memory, consciousness, individuality, and the essential or real self. Personality is connected to the soul but changes from life to life, dependent on sex, parents, health, and environment. In myriad ways, spirit uses the soul, which uses the personality (and body) of each life to grow and evolve, on its journey back to Oneness with its source.

Spirit, soul and personality resemble a light hanging

from the ceiling. The shade symbolises the personality, the bulb the soul and the inner spark of light (the electric filament) the spirit. Without the bulb the inner light would not be visible. Without the shade it would be blinding to look directly into the light.

I believe that all souls (embodying spirit) were created at the same time – although many have never incarnated into a physical body. What we on earth refer to as 'new souls' are not so much newly created as new to the experience of physical incarnation. (It is also possible that if a soul can sub-divide itself – rather as we can have children – the divided parts may be referred to as 'new' souls although they are in fact a part of the original.) 'Old' souls are those who have had numerous earthly, and other, lives, and who consciously encompass the totality of these experiences. 'Young' souls are those who have incarnated on earth very few times.

At first Yul-Han thought of the child only as his son, a part of himself, a third with Induk. As time passed, however, a most strange Prescience took hold of Yul-Han's mind and spirit . . . He perceived that the child had an old soul. It was not to be put in words, this meaning of an old soul. Yul-Han, observing the child, saw in his behaviour a reasonableness, a patience, a comprehension that was totally unchildlike. He did not scream when his food was delayed, as other infants do. Instead, his eyes calm and contemplative, he seemed to understand and was able to wait . . .

PEARL BUCK, *The Living Read*

Two or three years after I began to use regression therapy, a fairly well-known psychiatrist John Arnold (not his real name) asked me for an appointment. Somewhat hesitantly

– because I feared he would analyse and compare what I did with his own more scientific training – I agreed to see him.

Our session turned into a unique experience for us both. Having covered the ups and downs of John's present life, we went back into the past. Because I was apprehensive of how easy or difficult this might be for him, I spent longer guiding him into a relaxed state than I would normally. I took John backwards through birth, his time in the womb, conception and his pre-incarnation plans before suggesting that he look for a life that still in some way affected his present one.

Five minutes later, in a very drowsy voice, John said: 'I can't see anything, but what I'm feeling is quite incredible. I'm as small as a grain of sand, and yet as big as if the whole universe were contained inside me. I'm completely at one with myself and everything else. I've never experienced anything like this in my life before . . .' His voice trailed away.

John's feelings were so intense that both I and John's colleague who had come with him to observe the session sensed the change in the room's atmosphere. We felt bathed in a rosy glow and part of the peace and oneness John had described.

Our peace did not last long. Cries and wails of anguish suddenly filled the room. John thrashed about on the bed so violently that I thought he would fall off. As his movements gradually subsided he began to sob in a way that was far more disturbing than his previous cries. It was at least 30 minutes before John was able to speak. Even then his voice was almost inaudible. He told us he had gone back in time to the memory of being one with the Source of all life. John was initially so comfortable there that he wanted to remain for ever. But he began to feel the energy around him move and turn. It was slow at first, but gathered speed until he felt as if he were spinning like a revolving top, faster and faster, until he spun off and out into space and (what John described as) outer darkness. His shock, terror, pain of separation, sense of betrayal – 'I didn't do anything to deserve this' – reduced John to a whimpering wreck. It was as if he were a young child cast out from home too soon, abandoned by his parents, and left to fend for himself without any explanation or guidance.

Just as John's colleague and I had experienced his joy, so now we shared his grief. We also saw where some of the insecurity, guilt and lack of self-worth – which most of us suffer from to some extent or another – might have originated.

Eventually I asked John to try and describe his consciousness as he sensed it in its first stages of individualisation. He said that after his shock at his 'expulsion from the oneness' (which is what a baby feels at birth) he seemed to be a fragment of sound, like a musical note blown on the wind. Gradually he began to feel the need to create something around him, and this need caused his consciousness to expand. John went on to describe various stages of growth, through which he became increasingly aware and self-conscious.

Before I met John I understood that our first earthly experiences had to be those of observers rather than participants. As we evolve in intelligence and understanding, we incarnate into a physical body, through which we can then consciously participate in life. Today many 'new-to-planet-earth-souls' get their observer experience in bodies that suffer from cerebral palsy, Down's Syndrome, autism, mental retardation, paralysis or other life-restricting diseases. (Of course, this is not the sole reason for such problems.)

As John described his own evolving consciousness, it

seemed to fit this theory. At the same time, much of his evolution took place in between lives, as well as on other planes. In fact, it seems that incarnation in human form plays a relatively small part in our overall development. (Robert Monroe, who runs a research institute in America, which both teaches and investigates OBEs (out of body experiences) says that many of his subjects have seen that a soul can have different bodies existing at the same time – old, young, male, female. Nor are they limited to the earth plane, but may be simultaneously in different bodies in different planes. In fact, one of Monroe's subjects described a portion of himself as a 'slimy gelatine thing, living a life thousands of light years away'.

When John left my flat he said that he would never be able to practise psychiatry in quite the same way again. His analysis of his patients must now cover a far broader spectrum than he ever dreamed existed.

My understanding is that initially we begin our separation from God as tiny specks of consciousness which through myriad experiences get bigger and increasingly creative. As we evolve into human form we develop a personality which, with every lifetime, changes and expands. As the experiences of each life become part of our soul, mind and memory, so in turn does our soul consciousness expand. Eventually this becomes too big to be contained within one personality and one life, so it divides into fragments.

This means that after a number of human incarnations each individual contains only a fragment, or portion, of his total self. The rest of his consciousness, his other or alternative selves, co-exist, but in different realities and dimensions. In other words, as souls we inhabit simultaneously multidimensional realities, and live two, three, four or more lives at once.

For example, my self personality as Soozi Holbeche is now incarnate on the earth. Within this expression, my self appears complete, as a rose on a rosebush is a complete flower, but at the same time is only a part of and is *not* the complete rosebush. Meanwhile the other flowers on the rosebush lead their own individual lives, though interconnected by the same roots.

According to Seth, the discarnate entity channelled by Jane Roberts, author of many 'Seth books', 'various incarnational selves can be superficially regarded as portions of a crossword puzzle, for they are all portions of the whole, and yet can exist separately.' (Jane Roberts's books on the 'Education of Oversoul Seven' brilliantly illustrate this concept.) Richard Bach in his book *The Bridge Across Forever* writes about his alternate or possible selves – the characters he might have become if he had followed a different path, and who continue to exist 'just around a corner in time'.

Soul-mates And Soul Families

The Bridge Across Forever is really a love-story in which Bach (who also wrote *Jonathan Livingston Seagull* and *The Reluctant Messiah*) describes his desperate – and finally successful – search for the magical, mystical woman of his dreams and imagination – his soul-mate.

In the world today there are literally thousands of men and women involved in exactly the same pursuit. Whether young (some are barely out of kindergarten), old, or middle-aged, they ceaselessly search for their one true love in the form of a soul-mate.

Most people think of soul-mates as either the other half of themselves, or lovers from long ago. Our other half is a twin soul, sometimes known as a twin flame. Twin souls rarely incarnate together unless they are either at the end of a particular cycle of evolution, or have a specific – and usually spiritual – task to accomplish. It is a form of Divine economy that while one twin sojourns on the earth the other is free to explore a different dimension. When the earthly incarnation ends the two halves blend their various experiences together. (The best way to contact a twin soul or flame is through inner work such as meditation, dreams and visualisation. However, it is initially more important to develop a good and balanced relationship with one's inner self.)

Twin souls are in such perfect harmony that if on earth together there would be little opportunity for growth. They would literally think and be as one. (No matter how separate we may feel from this during our present incarnation we can at least look forward to it for the future!) Most of our close human relationships are those of personality rather than soul. These provide the greatest opportunities for growth and change. A personality relationship can be between any combination of people from husband and wife to friends or co-workers. Through them we press one another's buttons and gradually rub the edges off. Hopefully, as in the story of the *Velveteen Rabbit* by Margery Williams, we eventually become real.

Soul-mates are sometimes mistaken for twin souls because of the instant sense of recognition, connection and compatibility we have with them. A soul-mate is someone we have known for many lives – similar to a very old and dear friend with whom we feel completely at ease.

Today many of our this-life friendships are falling apart – either through physical separation or mental/emotional estrangement. At the same time we meet others with whom we have this immediate sense of bonding. As we move into the next millennium soul-mates are being drawn together as if on the end of invisible strings, to help and support one another.

Soul-mates, like members of soul families, often agree to incarnate together. However, soul-mates are usually there to provide a little comfort – a shoulder to cry on, or a helping hand when the going gets tough. By contrast, a member of our soul family can (though of course this is not always so) be part of a pre-incarnation plan to stimulate the very difficulties a soul-mate, by simply being around, helps us to face.

For example, my Karma suggests I need to feel what it is like to be bullied. A soul family member – *because he loves me enough to help me to evolve* – incarnates to act out the bully. Incarnate myself, I usually forget this plan, and blame the very person who is trying to help me, for being so nasty. In fact, the people whose actions and personalities cause us the most trauma are usually the ones who – from a soul point of view – love us the most. (Sometimes a soul will choose to incarnate as what is known as a catalyst disciple. A catalyst disciple will tend to have either an abrasive or a very powerful personality that automatically stimulates reaction, and subsequent change, without any specific effort on his part.)

Soul families, aside from playing the 'baddie' when necessary, also help one another to understand every facet of human love. This means that they will take it in turns to incarnate as mothers, fathers, brothers, sisters, grandparents, grandchildren, nieces, nephews, aunts, uncles, cousins, lovers, neighbours and friends, over and over again, until each family member is totally familiar with human love and emotion. This does not mean that every man, woman and child in our present and physically incarnated family is automatically part of our soul family. In fact, most human families today consist of people gathered together to work out last bits and pieces of Karma, Karmic debts and responsibilities, before the end of the century. Once this has been done, there is no longer any need to stay together. This is one reason for the apparent breakdown of family life.

Neither is a soul group the same as a soul family. A soul group usually comprises a number of kindred spirits who incarnate at the same time to help one another accomplish the same task. Another type of soul group is that formed from the common interest of religion, politics, country, experience and hobbies – or resistance to all of them. The energy of attachment to, or resistance against, will automatically draw those concerned together.

Walk-ins And Other Advanced Souls

Aside from twin souls, soul-mates, group souls and others, we also have 'walk-ins'. A genuine walk-in is a highly evolved soul who, by prior arrangement, literally takes over, or moves into, an already formed human body. In America I met a number of men and women who claimed to be walk-ins. The only one I really believed in was a woman – Marina.

Marina told me she had adopted the body and person-ality of 39-year-old Antonia Dobbs, a talented interior designer from Texas, who had nearly died in a car crash, and was on a life-support machine for two weeks. That was when Marina took over Antonia's body and all her responsibilities, including her interior design business and her bedridden 86-year-old mother.

Antonia's business partner was her ex-husband Leonard. Marina (as Antonia) convinced him to buy out full control of the business. Two months later he rang to beg her to help him with an enormous project. As she would have absolutely no idea what to do, she refused. He insisted. But indeed she made such a disaster that she finally told him that she was not really Antonia but a walk-in. Initially incredulous, Leonard ultimately believed Marina and has over the years given her much support.

Walk-ins choose to take over human bodies, while their real owners leave, in order to cut out the slow process of growth from baby-to-child-to-adolescent-to-young-adult. Only an avatar or a highly-trained initiate would be permitted – or even have the skill – to carry out such an exercise. When a soul incarnates as a result of conception, pregnancy and birth, his energy spirals downwards towards his future parents. Their sexual relationship in turn beams a spiral of energy towards the soul preparing to enter. The two spirals intertwine, creating a funnel through which the soul descends.

En route the soul puts on *in consciousness* (almost like an actor trying on clothes for a particular performance) the mental, emotional and physical bodies he has chosen for his next life. Often at this point a soul says: 'I didn't realize that the bodies I chose would feel so bad!' (He may, for example, have chosen a mind that lacks intelligence, emotions that are excruciatingly sensitive, and a body with a leg or arm missing.) 'I won't be able to cope!' This then triggers another level of insecurity, fear and lack of self-trust which is why so many of us feel we were lacking in self-esteem from the moment we were born.

Six weeks before conception, the entering soul is in place within his future mother's auric field, which now doubles in size. From here he gives both parents little reminding nudges of his presence. After conception he stays around to keep an eye on the growth of the developing foetus.

A walk-in bypasses all of this and has to enter through the planetary ring-pass-not that encircles the earth a bit like a spiritual ozone layer. Walk-ins are usually spiritual teachers/healers, and come back to earth to help humanity during certain key phases of evolution. Today they are here to help us move more easily into the next millennium. A genuine walk-in is an advanced soul. Therefore the light he shines, as he begins to penetrate the earth's atmosphere, draws to him negativity which must be overcome and transformed before he can assume another person's body. This is why he must be a highly evolved soul.

In the far distant future we shall all come and go from the earth plane as we please. Without the dense physical bodies we have today, we shall simply decrease our vibratory rate to enter the earth's plane, and increase it to move elsewhere, somewhat like changing gears in a car.

The kind of personality change resulting from traumas, such as illness, death, divorce, change of job or move to another country, does not automatically imply a 'walk-in-situation'. A walk-in is fully cognisant of who he is and what he is here to do. If genuine, he would never advertise: 'I'm a walk-in!' (Marina and I only discussed *her* situation because of specific spiritual work we did together.)

It is also important to remember that a walk-in is in no way like a possessive entity. The latter attempts to control a personality by seduction or force, rather than by prior agreement. (I shall discuss possession in more detail in the next chapter.)

In addition to the wide range of soul types in existence, we also have archangels, angels, discarnate spirit guides, teachers and helpers. Archangels and angels, although always available to help us, never incarnate in physical form. (Unless it's a 'fallen angel'!) Spirit guides, teachers and helpers have had many incarnations, and know exactly what it is like to inhabit a human body. Their challenge is to help us face and overcome the challenges life presents (which are in fact self-created). As we evolve, so do they. As they graduate, we shall replace them, and lend a similar helping hand to those a few steps behind us.

The Seven Planes

Between our first and last earthly incarnations we must pass through many planes. A plane denotes a particular level of consciousness. There are basically seven planes which correspond to the chakras in our bodies – however, there are 49 levels to each plane, so we do not automatically zoom from lower to higher planes with each new lifetime.

The chakras are vital energy centres which connect to the spine by cords. They control the organs and glands of the body and relate to different frequencies on the colour scale. For example, the root or base chakra controls the gonads, the spleen or sacral chakra the adrenals, the solar plexus (at the diaphragm) the pancreas, the heart the thymus, the throat the thyroid, the third eye (in the centre of the forehead) the pituitary, and the crown the pineal.

The inner planes to which each chakra relates are as follows: the root chakra relates to the etheric plane, and the spleen to the lower astral, which is the plane of instinctual emotion and desire. The solar plexus relates to the higher astral – a plane of altruistic emotion, in other words, the desire to help others. The heart relates to the lower or concrete mental – a plane of fixed beliefs. We even say: 'As a man thinketh in his heart, so he is.' People who get stuck on this plane become the fanatics who believe that their way is the only way. The throat relates to the upper mental or causal plane, and the third eye to the lower spiritual – where we find angels, guides and teachers. The crown relates to the plane of pure spirit and oneness with God.

Each plane presents different opportunities for growth, just as our schools, from pre-school to university, teach different grades of lesson. The first plane could be compared to pre-school, the second to kindergarten, the third to primary school, the fourth to high school, the fifth to college or university, the sixth to taking a Master's degree, and the seventh to putting all we have learned into practice. The first four planes are to do with self-consciousness. The last three move us into cosmic consciousness.

Because the planes merge and overlap, we often move through other realms without even recognising it. An illustration of two dimensions briefly blending together is the story of friends who, as they walked through Hyde Park on a summer's afternoon, suddenly heard voices above their heads. Looking up, they saw three young women in animated conversation, strolling about in the air as if they were passing through a park. The image lasted for ten minutes and then faded. The young women seemed totally unaware of my friends below.

As soul fragments, not only do we have to experience every facet of every plane, but we must also explore the qualities of every colour and every ray.

The colour of the first ray is red, and its qualities are of will, power, spontaneity, initiative and leadership. The second ray's qualities are those of blue, signifying love, wisdom, compassion and gentleness. The third ray is yellow, which is to do with mental ability, the power to organise, evaluate and administer. The fourth ray is green, which is the colour of unconditional love, acceptance, forgiveness and co-operation with others. The fifth ray is orange, which is the colour of emotional courage, analysis, loyalty and relatedness to others. The sixth, or violet-purple ray, is the one of duty, responsibility, spiritual devotion, wisdom and grace. The seventh ray is indigo, whose qualities are inspiration, aspiration, balance, humanitarianism, and service.

Each ray also has its negative side. For example, the negative aspects of green are jealousy, meanness, envy, pessimism and possessiveness. The negative side of an orange ray person is that he may be too dependent on what others think. He may be indecisive, and procrastinate, seethe with pent-up emotion, while being very critical of others.

We enter each lifetime on a different ray, and so learn the positive and negative qualities of each. As we near the end of the century, most of us are here to balance the qualities of all the rays together, as if we were human rainbows.

During our various earthly lifetimes we also have many lessons that go from I am, I have, I think, I feel, I will, I analyse, I balance, I create, I perceive, I use, I serve, to I synthesise and integrate all I have learned. The first three are to do with self-awareness, the second three relate to the family, the seventh, eighth and ninth are connected to others (beyond family) and the final three are to do with our interaction with the world.

When I was at school I had the impression that I was living my third and final life. After my discoveries of Karma, inner and outer planes, the chakras, rays, colours, the twelve challenges presented by each astrological sign, together with the multitudinous reasons for incarnation, I now think I would be lucky to get away with a mere 3000 lives.

Our soul purpose for incarnation on this or other planets (although 'to incarnate' on another planet may not be the correct expression) is reunion with God. Our life purpose is how we do it. We might argue that if all we've done for billions of years is to try to find our way back to the source of all life, with whom we were originally one, what was the point of separation in the first place? The answer is clear in the story of the prodigal son, told in St Luke's gospel.

A man had two sons: the younger said to his father: 'Give me the portion of goods that falleth to me' and his father duly handed over his younger son's inheritance. The boy left home and wasted it all in riotous living. Suddenly a terrible famine hit the country to which he had moved. The younger son, now penniless, hungry and desperate, found a job feeding pigs. Half dead from starvation, he remembered how well his father's servants were fed and, full of remorse, decided to return home, beg his father's forgiveness, and offer to work in the house as a servant.

Instead of berating his younger son, the father was delighted to see him back. He arranged a huge welcome-home party, with fatted calf, music and dancing. The elder son was upset, and said: 'Lo, these many years do I serve thee, neither transgressed I at any time thy commandment; and yet thou never gavest me a kid, that I might make merry with my friends.'

The key point to this story is that the elder son serves his father because it is expected of him, and he knows nothing else. The younger son (after his adventures) serves his father because he now values what his father represents, and chooses to do so. The father in the parable represents God. The story tells us that in the process of individuation we must leave our Father's house – and journey through multiple experiences, in which we usually identify with creation instead of the spirit behind creation. Eventually our sense of separation from the Oneness (which no other experience can totally assuage) draws us back to 'Our Father's house', but now with creative self-conscious awareness, and not as blind puppets.

It is as if I have lived all my life in a blue room. Because I have never seen anything else, I do not even know what blue is. One day I leave my blue room and am astonished to discover many other colours. I now see blue for what it is, because I have these other colours with which to compare it.

In the same way, when we were one we neither knew nor appreciated it. After experiencing separation and duality, we finally want nothing more than to return to the Oneness. We do not return empty-handed, but take with us wisdom and enlightenment.

I seem to understand as never before how the mystery that is called the soul of me must have quickened in every form of past existence, and must as certainly continue to behold the sun for other millions of summers, through eyes of other countless shapes of future beings . . .

LAFCADIO HEARN

8

DEATH –
INBETWEEN LIVES –
PREPARATION FOR BIRTH

I died as a mineral and became a plant,
I died as a plant and rose to animal,
I died as animal and I was Man.
Why should I fear? When was I less by dying?
Yet once more I shall die as a Man, to soar
With angels blest; but even from angelhood
I must pass on . . .

JALALU'L EL-DIN RUMI (1207–73)

The basic principle of past-life therapy is to extricate from a person's unconscious or subconscious phobias, feelings and memories that stem from the past. These can then be healed and integrated so that they no longer have any power over the personality. Usually the mere re-living dissipates them.

One of the most common fears or phobias – which seems to affect nearly 80 per cent of the world's population – is the fear of death and dying. In regression therapy this fear can be assuaged when the subject is asked to describe and re-live the dying moments of many of their past lives.

Death Re-lived

For example, Madeleine was not afraid of death itself, but of the manner in which death might occur. Already suffering from asthma, Madeleine was afraid of choking and gasping for air when her last moments came.

During a session, Madeleine saw that she had suffocated to death not once but three times in other lives. As she remembered these deaths she said: 'I'm not even in my body. I'm looking down on myself and I see my body convulsed as it tries to breathe – but it doesn't matter. I'm not there any more.' Madeleine's relief when she realised that, even if her body died from an asthma attack, she herself would not suffer, helped to reduce the severity and frequency of the attacks.

Lily, who today is a medical student, saw her life as a young London prostitute in the mid 1800s, cut short by murder. She described herself as a very pretty, flirtatious and somewhat silly girl, who took to prostitution more from laziness than lust. She was good-natured, had lots of friends, both men and women, and, when not working, liked nothing better than to accompany them to the local music-hall.

One night, as Lily walked home alone, a man whose advances she had spurned followed and killed her. Lily's description of her last walk down dimly-lit steps on a dark night with the sound of rapidly-approaching feet behind her, reminded me of stories of Jack the Ripper. Afraid to run, she paused for a moment and hoped that whoever was there would walk on past her.

Instead, Lily felt hands grab her round her neck. She fell. Her murderer kicked and pushed her to the bottom of the steps and stuck a knife in her heart. The fear in Lily's voice, as she described her pre-death moments, completely and amazingly changed to peace when she said: 'He forced the knife into my heart. Even then he wasn't satisfied. He went on kicking my body before he finally threw it into the river. If he could only see how pointless his killing was. For I'm free! I'm sorry I mocked and insulted him, because I realise now that this stimulated him to kill me. But even when I see my body kicked, beaten and abused I feel no pain. For some reason my life, although it appears cut short, fulfilled a plan. I'm floating above my body and must go with those who are here to greet me.'

I asked Lily if she ever forgave her murderer. She replied: 'There's nothing to forgive. On a certain level this death was a pre-ordained part of my spiritual education. Maybe if I had physically experienced the pain of the knife entering my heart it would be different, but I simply watched it happening as if it were nothing at all to do with me.'

'Consuelo,' he said to her, '. . . I am going to leave you for a time and then I shall return to earth by means of a new birth . . .'

GEORGE SAND, *The Ring of Return*

Joe saw himself, two or three hundred years ago, drowned in a flood which suddenly swallowed up his family and their land. To watch his face and listen to his words as he cried: 'The water's coming through the door! I'm alone!' sent chills up my spine. 'My mother and father have gone for help. They left me behind because they thought I'd be safe. But the water won't stop! I've put furniture against the door, but it doesn't stop the water coming in. Now it's up to my knees! I stand on a chair, then a table. I scream for help!' Sweat and tears rolled down Joe's cheeks as he recounted his experience. The water came up to his neck, ears and eyes. Like Lily, Joe's voice became very quiet when he described his final moments.

'What's happening, Joe?' I asked.

'It's all right,' he replied. 'As the water rose above my head I floated out of the window and it didn't matter any more.'

'Was there any pain?'

'No. I was afraid of the water when it came through the door, but it didn't hurt me. I seemed to lift out of the top of my head and watch the water rise to the ceiling. It was as if I were there and not there at the same time.'

Joe also remembered a military life in which he was shot on a battlefield. Not realising he was dead, Joe continued to fight until he saw that his efforts made no physical impression on his enemy. I asked Joe what he learned from that life, and he said: 'To kill is a terrible and violent act. To kill what you hate attaches you to what you hate.'

Annie, in another life, committed suicide. In her session she said: 'Although there's no condemnation here for what I did, I now see that I face the same problems that I tried to avoid on earth. I am full of guilt for the pain I caused my family and friends, but my death was easy. I simply put my body to sleep with drugs and alcohol and lifted out of it. It was far worse for the people who later found me. In fact, their pain holds me back and keeps me where I am now.' (Annie appeared to describe an immediate after-death, lower-astral plane.)

After a few moments Annie went on: 'I can now laugh at what drove me to end this other life. I see that I created my own problems in order to overcome them. Next time around I shall value each moment and live my life to the full, instead of passing through it like an uninvited guest.'

Sam, who was 19 when he landed on my doorstep, lived in terror of not fulfilling his life's purpose.

He re-experienced his most recent death as that of a

three-day-old baby. When I asked Sam what he had learned from such a very brief visit to earth, he replied: 'I discovered what it was like to have my expression stifled.' Apparently, in another past life Sam had been a powerful dictator. In order to control the people around him, he blocked them from developing their full potential. To die so young was Sam's chosen way of facing that particular Karma. He added that his parents then grieved over his death, not because he was who he was – after all, they barely knew him – but for their 'lost hopes and expectations'. It seems that, as much as Sam came in to learn his own lessons, he was also a teacher. He said that his death was painless, and added that parents of babies and children who die young should remember that their souls or spiritual selves are not three days, three months, or three years old, but ageless.

Jenny Green (whose life as Dorothy Helman I mention in Chapter 4) described herself, a few minutes before death, as being 'a shadow standing next to Dorothy, so that Dorothy should not be alone'. She had no immediate sense of being dead, and spoke as if she and Dorothy were two separate people. Eventually she said: 'I've got to go! I don't want to leave her (Dorothy's body) all alone, but I'm being pulled up. I can't stay.' Peter Ramsder, the hypnotist, guided Jenny to let herself go, and see what happened next. Jenny, tears rolling down her cheeks, suddenly sat up and opened her arms as if to embrace someone. 'Poppa – Poppa!' she cried. 'Why did you leave me?' Later, Jenny said she no longer had any fear of death.

When Gwen McDonald, as Rose Duncan (also in Chapter 4), was asked to describe Rose's death, a look of pure joy spread across her face. 'I'm standing on a path leading through a field of wild flowers. The colours are so beautiful! A woman in a white dress is coming towards me. I've never seen her before, but I feel as if I know her.

She takes my arm and leads me into a big white building.'
Gwen's voice trailed away. When pushed to describe, in
physical terms, how Rose's life ended, she was completely
uninterested: 'Oh, she's lying on a bed, but what's it
matter? She was ready to go.' Again, there was a sense of
Gwen being out of Rose's body, and seeing it like an
outworn winter coat.

Sally and Veronica both burned to death in other lives,
Sally as a so-called witch during the Inquisition, Veronica
in a house that was accidentally set on fire. They both
spoke of their terror as the flames approached, but again
the moment of actual transition from physical to spiritual
body appeared to take place without pain or difficulty.

I recently watched a research programme in which
about twenty children who claimed memories of other
lives were asked to describe, under hypnosis, how those
lives came to an end. While many spoke of fear and panic
caused by the circumstances surrounding these deaths, all
of them described death itself as no more difficult than
taking off a pair of tight shoes. They had a sense of
freedom, expansion and release.

Out of trance, these children also claimed to have no
fear of death, nor of the manner in which death might
come. One had seen himself die through falling off a cliff,
another witnessed his death in a plane crash, and a third
was shot as a policeman. In each case it seemed that the
essential or spiritual self moved out of the body before
death occurred. (Three to seven days before death, the
aura or electromagnetic field round the body disappears,
which illustrates the same process.)

Near-Death Experience

Descriptions of near-death experiences (NDEs) are almost identical to those of past-life deaths. They too alleviate the fear of dying. In the past, esoteric schools and healing temples addressed this fear by initiating their students into the act of dying by teaching them how to leave their bodies at will. This gave the students a deep sense of security, as they knew that no matter how they died they would not suffer. Today an NDE is the modern equivalent of such an initiation. Those who have experienced one usually gain a sense of spiritual indestructibility, a wider view of life, and an awareness that being genuinely human has nothing to do with having wealth or material success.

In the video *Visions of Hope* made by IANDS, an organisation set up to investigate NDEs, a number of people who have had these experiences tell their stories.

One man 'died' in a hospital ward and woke up on a trolley and covered by a sheet in the hospital morgue. He said: 'I woke up as the morgue attendant walked towards me. He fainted. My mother told me I must always be nice to others, so I got off the trolley to help him. I knelt beside him on the floor and patted his face. He opened his eyes and fainted again when he saw what he thought was a corpse leaning over him.' He added: 'I must say, I didn't feel too good myself!' (Which must be one of the greatest understatements of all time.)

This same man also described how he lifted out of his body and saw that he was still connected to it by a silvery cord, similar to an umbilical cord. He broke it, and suddenly found himself in a room full of people where someone he thought was Jesus patted him on the shoulder and said: 'Go back. It's not your time.' At this point he returned to his body.

A young Jewish boy died in bed at home. At ease and floating above his body, he heard the doctor tell his parents: 'I'm sorry, the little lad as gone.' The doctor added that a post-mortem must be done immediately to clarify why the boy had died. Because the family was strictly orthodox and it was a Friday night, they refused to give their permission to tamper with the body until the following Monday. On Sunday the boy 'came alive again'. Through this experience he has become a counsellor, healer and workshop leader.

A 35-year-old married woman developed severe meningitis and was rushed into hospital. Watching her body in the narrow hospital bed she felt herself float to the ceiling, 'Like a balloon cut free of its string'. Quite happy to float, she suddenly became aware of her husband 'sobbing across her stomach' and her two very young sons looking lost and confused beside him. Their emotional pain pulled her back into her body and forced her to continue a physical life.

Another woman, at the end of her story, looked radiant as she said: 'I'm not afraid to die. In fact I'm actually looking forward to it.'

An eight-year-old boy who fell into a river while fishing was pronounced dead by the policeman who pulled him out. Despite the policeman's frantic efforts to resuscitate him, the ambulance men also reported the boy dead when they arrived to take him to hospital. Two days later he revived and described every detail of what had occurred during and after his rescue. When asked how he knew he replied: 'I watched everything from outside my body.'

In Shirley MacLaine's book *Out On A Limb* she describes a conversation with Peter Sellers in which he tells her of his own brush with death. Peter said: 'I felt myself leave my body. I just floated out of my physical form and I saw them cart my body away to the hospital.

I went with it. I was curious. I wondered what was wrong with me. I wasn't frightened or anything like that because I was fine, and it was my body that was in trouble.' The actor then described how his doctor did everything he could to get his heart beating again, including on-the-spot surgery, in which he took Seller's heart out of his body and tried to massage it back to life.

'At this point,' said Sellers, 'I looked around myself and saw an incredibly beautiful bright burning white light above me. I wanted to go to that white light more than anything. I knew there was love, real love, on the other side of the light that attracted me so much. Then I saw a hand reach through the light. I tried to touch it, to grab onto it, to clasp it so it could sweep me up and pull me through it. Then I heard Rex (the doctor) say below me: "It's beating again. I'm getting a heart beat." At the same moment a voice attached to the hand I wanted to touch said: "It's not time. Go back and finish. It's not time . . ."'

Peter Sellers ended his story by saying that he knew he'd lived many times before, and that this experience confirmed it for him, because: 'in *this* lifetime I felt what it was for my soul to be actually out of my body.'

Two or three years ago *Reader's Digest* did a series of articles on NDEs. During their investigation they found that no matter how a person nearly died – fell off a mountain, drowned in a boating or scuba-diving accident, suffocated in a pot-hole, had a heart-attack – the out-of-body experiences were very similar. They watched what was happening to their bodies with almost clinical disinterest, and almost without exception had no desire to return to them.

In the video *Visions of Hope*, Elizabeth Kübler-Ross (herself a doctor and psychiatrist) said words to the effect of: 'How can doctors say these experiences are hallucinations caused by drugs or brain damage when a totally blind person who is pronounced dead and later revives, describes to me the clothes I am wearing and what the nurses talked about at the end of the corridor? Since my own near-death experience I know that life continues out of, or beyond, the body. You can hang me by my toenails and I'll still say it is true. Those who don't believe will find it for themselves at the end.'

Research has shown that when an area of the brain known as the Sylvian fissure (located in the right temporal lobe) is stimulated with an electric probe it can cause out-of-body sensations similar to an NDE. However, there is no awareness of the light, which seems to be a key element in all genuine NDEs. Dr Melvin Morse says: 'If this light is only a spasm of rigor mortis of the optic nerve, how can we account for the love, peace and joy described by NDE subjects?'

Dr Ritchie, an American doctor and psychiatrist, spoke of his own NDE and the light he saw, in the following words: 'I stared in astonishment as the brightness increased, coming from nowhere, seeming to shine everywhere at once. All the light-bulbs in the ward couldn't give off that much light. All the light-bulbs in the world couldn't. It was like a million welders' lamps all blazing at once.' Dr Ritchie then saw that it was not just light but a man of light who came into the room. The power of light and love emanating from this man – 'who knew everything unloveable about me, yet accepted and loved me just the same' – changed Ritchie's life. He was also asked: 'What have you done with your life?' which made him realise that he had done very little. Ritchie was literally transformed by the light of this experience, as are most NDE subjects. This does not happen as a result of artificially induced OBEs (out of body experiences), nor is it experienced by those who attempt suicide.

Suicide

Most resuscitated suicide survivors describe finding themselves in a dark, unpleasant place in which they feel enveloped in the misery they have caused their family and friends. Maria, revived from an overdose of sleeping tablets, told me that it was like being trapped alone in a thick impenetrable fog in which she was still stuck to the problems from which she had tried to escape. She saw now that there was no such way out, and that it would have been easier to deal with these problems while still in a physical body. Maria also realised that her difficulties had not been insurmountable, but rather a challenge to grow and evolve. 'I know now that even if my life is not easy, all I have to do is the best I can,' said Maria.

Jack cut his wrists, and lost so much blood that the hospital did not expect him to recover. He said: 'I found myself in a very dark, noisy place which seemed like a disused basement, full of cobwebs which brushed across my face. At the beginning I could see nothing, but I heard people groaning and sobbing. After what seemed like aeons of time the darkness lifted a little, and I saw my mother and family grieving over my death. I moved towards her and told her over and over again that I was truly sorry for the pain I caused her.' His desperation when he realised that she could neither see nor hear him made him wish that he had not taken his own life. At this point he suddenly returned to his body with the realisation that life was precious and that he must make full use of the opportunities available to him.

Dr Ritchie, during his own NDE, saw people attempting to communicate in vain with those they had left behind. 'Please forgive me, Dad, I didn't mean to hurt you.' 'I'm sorry Mum . . . Please try to understand.' He wondered why these people continued to talk to others who could neither see nor hear them. Suddenly he heard a voice say: 'They are suicides, chained to the consequences of their acts.'

People who either attempt or in fact do commit suicide appear to go initially to a sort of murky grey twilight zone. We can help them by visualising an image of them, as they were at the healthiest, happiest time of their lives, surrounded by and filled with light. We can think and talk of the happiness their lives brought to their families and friends. We can imagine saying to them, in our minds: 'Maybe I don't understand why you took your own life, but it's all right – I accept that you made your own choice, and I love you for who you are, not for what you do or do not do.' If there is any need to forgive, do this at the same time. Light, love, and true whole-hearted acceptance can transform this grey twilight zone and help the suicide victim to move out of it.

In an article in *US Today* (1984), concerning suicide and attempted suicide amongst adolescents, the National Center for Health Statistics reports that suicides have quadrupled since 1980. Other experts believe that the true number is at least double this. Mary Susan Miller, a child educator and expert on suicide, said that adolescent suicides have increased 20 per cent. These reports were written eleven years ago, and the latest figures have again increased drastically. It is as if there is a world-wide epidemic, which we need to counteract by teaching what happens after a person takes his own life.

The good news is that reports by Dr Bruce Greyson at the University of Michigan Medical Center say that attempted suicides who have been resuscitated 'Come out with a real sense of purpose in their lives. Death is no longer fearful, life has become more meaningful.' In the words of T. S. Eliot: 'It is worth dying to find out what life is.'

Fear Of Death

Jung wrote: 'Death is just as psychologically important as birth.' Indigenous people accept birth and death as part of the continuing cycle of creation. Most Westerners fear death and see it as an unnatural and catastrophic event.

Instead of being taught to accept death as inevitable and the act of dying as a mere shift from one level of consciousness to another (in fact, a physical death is a spiritual birth, and vice versa), we learn, almost from birth, to think of death as a fatal and unmentionable disease which must be discussed behind closed doors – and certainly not in front of the children.

An example of this is what happened to Inge, a very dear friend of mine. Inge was 15 years old and at boarding-school when her father unexpectedly died of a heart attack. Her mother, without telling Inge or the school what had happened, arranged for Inge to stay at the school for the next two school holidays. Inge's father was an actor, which meant that her parents frequently travelled, so Inge accepted this arrangement without question. Six months later she arrived home to be told of her father's death. The shock of the news, the sense of having been betrayed by her mother, who, from a misguided desire to protect her daughter, had put off telling her of her father's death and not allowed her to mourn at his funeral, affected Inge emotionally for the rest of her life. Initially she searched the streets for her father, unable to believe that he could disappear so completely. Death became something fearful and incomprehensible. Even as an adult, she told me that she sometimes saw in the distance a man who reminded her of her father, and would rush up to greet him, only to find a stranger.

By contrast, another friend, Jenny, was with her father

when he died, and so was her three-year-old son Sam. Jenny's father lay peacefully in his bed, when Sam suddenly clambered up and patted his grandfather's cheeks, stroked his hair, held his hands and even lifted his eyelids. He was very gentle. He remarked to Jenny: 'Grandfather's very cold, but it doesn't matter, because he's not here any more, is he?' He added: 'We'll be like this one day, won't we?' Sam then left the room to return five minutes later with a daisy from the garden which he very carefully placed in his grandfather's hand. Completely satisfied, Sam went back to play with his toys. If all children could meet death in this way, they would have no fear, and would simply accept death as part of life.

Setting Free

Resistance to anything creates a barrier. Acceptance dissolves it. Resistance to death – our own or that of someone we love – can make it an unnecessarily traumatic experience. Acceptance that death is unavoidable, a new beginning rather than a final ending, makes it easy.

It is not the psychologist who must be questioned as to what happens finally to the detached consciousness. Whatever theoretical position he assumed, he would hopelessly overstep the boundaries of his scientific competence. He can only point out that the views of our text with respect to the timelessness of the detached consciousness are in harmony with the religious thought of all times, and with that of the overwhelming majority of mankind. He can say, further, that anyone who does not think this way would stand outside the human order, and would therefore be suffering from a disturbance to his psychic equilibrium. As a physician, then, I make the greatest effort to fortify, so far as I have the power, a belief in immortality, especially in my older patients to whom such questions are menacingly near.

C. J. JUNG

I have never heard of any NDE subject complaining of a struggle to leave his body. He was in it one minute and out of it the next. It seems that death is easier than birth. I certainly found this to be the case in my own NDE.

From this experience, combined with my work with doctors, psychiatrists, nurses and the terminally ill themselves, I understand the dying process to be somewhat like this: no matter how death occurs – sudden accident, prolonged illness, disease or trauma – the spirit begins to loosen its connection with the physical three to seven days before. When the body gives its final gasp, the essence of its owner is above or beside it looking on.

While most people lift – or even jump – out of the top of their heads, some release from the solar plexus or diaphragm. They then float around until 'the silver cord is loosed' (Ecclesiastes, 12:6) and their energy is transferred from the physical to the spiritual.

A doctor who witnessed his aunt's death, described seeing a hazy, fog-like substance suspended in the air about two feet above her bed. As he watched, this gradually solidified into the physical shape of his aunt. He then saw a silver cord running from her head to her spiritual double's head. It pulsed with energy. As his aunt's body diminished, the other astral or spirit body grew stronger and stronger. Finally the cord between the two snapped. The physical body sank back and 'died', while the other rose up, radiant and glowing, and left.

Doctors in Australia using infra-red cameras – both at the bed of dying patients and on the other side of the walls around the room – witnessed exactly the same phenomenon. The glowing light body lifted out, and increased in strength as the physical body died. It then floated through the walls – clearly enough to be picked up on camera.

It seems that immediately after a person's 'lift off' from a physical to a spiritual dimension, he is greeted by all those he has loved and been loved by. (Even if they are already reincarnated, they are there in consciousness at this time.) He is also welcomed by the light, love and presence of his own teachers and guides.

He hovers fairly close to the physical plane until after his funeral. During this time he is extremely sensitive to the emotions of those he has left behind, and will often try to reassure them (usually unsuccessfully) of his continued existence. A funeral should be a celebration of life rather than a mourning of departure, because the energy engendered by those present helps to lift the soul to its next level. If it is too mournful and sombre, the soul is dragged down.

For three days after a person's death it is fine to cry, scream and groan. After that it becomes selfish – a focus on 'How could you leave me like this?' 'How am I going to manage without you?' instead of 'I wish you well in your new life.'

No matter how much we may love the person whose time has come to move on, we must let him go, knowing that if we do not we interfere with his next experience. It is exactly the same as if my son goes from England to Australia and I telephone every day to say: 'I miss you so much; how are you? What are you doing, thinking, feeling, eating?' He is burdened by my anxiety, instead of free to enjoy a new country.

When we are unable to let go of someone who has died, it is usually because there is something unfinished that needs to be cleared. Maybe we need to forgive or be forgiven, say words that were forever unsaid, express an emotion continually bottled up.

There are numerous ways to do this from meditation and prayer, self-help workshops, discussion with friends or therapists, to seeing a doctor or psychologist.

I have also personally found the following techniques to be simple and effective. One is to write a letter to the person with whom I have a problem or whom I cannot release (whether dead or alive), in which I freely express what I have never said before. I then burn the letter in a fire or candle-flame, knowing that it will be received and understood, almost like a form of written prayer. This can also be done by visualising the person, and mentally communicating the same message. A quartz crystal or rutilated quartz held in the left hand adds power to this process. They act like a microphone or telephone, and help the message to get through more easily. Another way is to ask for a dream through which the relationship may be healed or completed. In this case a quartz crystal or rutilated quartz can be placed under the pillow. (Rutilated quartz has tiny silver or gold threads running through it, almost like miniature telephone wires, and can assist every type of communication.)

Sometimes I prefer to sit on the floor with a lighted candle and invoke the angels and guides of the person I wish to release or talk to. I ask for their help and guidance. This procedure is particularly helpful for parents of young children and babies who have died, as well as for those who have suffered a miscarriage or abortion. Release the soul, who perhaps made an exploratory visit to earth in preparation for a future return (or something else altogether) by saying words to the effect of: 'I'm sorry that it was not appropriate for you to stay with me or come through me at this time. I bless and release you with love, knowing that if we need to meet again in the future we shall do so.'

All of these procedures work better in an atmosphere of peace and light. Crystals, candles, flowers, incense, fragrant oils and herbs, soft music, help consciousness expand into a spiritual dimension.

It is not a good idea to go to clairvoyants, mediums and psychics in an attempt to call up the dead. It can disturb them. If someone you love wants to get through to you, he will, in his own way. The methods I describe are like popping a letter into the mail-box, and letting it go.

In Between Lives

Helen Wambach, the psychiatrist who specialised in past life research, said:

> *I think, as we die, that we go through a process of retaining fairly close identification with the personality we have last been on earth. The larger personality absorbs the recently experienced personality but discards the unimportant things such as race, social security numbers and belief systems. Then I believe that the soul or deeper self can plan a new expedition into physical reality in order to experience emotions, develop knowledge and, most important of all, to live with other souls so as to straighten out past mistakes.*

Before planning his next expedition to earth, however, the newly deceased must first get used to his astral or light body. This is initially similar to the image of the physical body he has just left, and is created by the way he has lived his life on earth. He must adapt to functioning in this body purely from the power of thought – as well as to the realisation that every thought he now has is clearly visible to those around him. (As a child I saw people's thoughts, and they never matched what was said, which was very confusing.)

On earth we are often told that we create our own reality by our thoughts. In other words, our experience is the direct result of our thinking – thought comes first, experience second. Once his initial separation from the physical plane is complete, the now astral personality will see exactly what he believes he will see. He faces his own thought forms, which is partly what the *Tibetan Book of the Dead* is about. If he believes in punishment or judgement he will see and experience that. If he believes that God is a giant lizard, he will see a giant lizard – and so on until he realises that he can recreate everything around him.

With the aid of teachers and guides, this person will also review his entire life from the perspective of being on the receiving end of every thought, word, deed and emotion which he initiated. He will feel, and understand exactly how he affected everyone and everything around him. This is not done as punishment, but to help him gain insight and self-knowledge for the future. He will also be shown how his own life fitted into a far greater picture, a universal plan.

Regression subjects, (and even some NDEs) who recall this review say that through it they learned that love was the only thing that really mattered, that whether we die young or old is less important than if we have lived our lives to the full; that we are totally responsible for who we are and what we do – in other words, no one else is going to save us, or do it for us.

I was hypnotized by her eyes and I had a complete vision of her as if she were in the room. Now I don't know if that had anything to do with what happened next, but I had a flash. I came to the realisation that I was responsible for my whole life, whatever had happened. I used to blame my family, society, my wife ... and that day I saw so clearly that I had nobody to blame but myself. I put everything on my own shoulders and I felt so relieved. Now I'm free, no one else is responsible.

HENRY MILLAR, Paris 1934, on seeing a photograph
of Mme Blavatsky

People who have a lot of regrets about what they have or have not done tend to die less easily and have greater difficulty after death. (If we have left a lot of things undone, or still feel regret for unfulfilled wishes and dreams, we can clear them out of the way by visualisation and imagination. In our mind's eye, we can see ourselves accomplishing anything and everything.)

Let us not reach the end of our lives with the sentiments expressed by 85-year-old Nadine Stair, who wrote:

If I had to live my life over again, I'd dare to make
*   more mistakes next time.*
I'd relax.
I would limber up.
I would be sillier than I have been on this trip.
I would take fewer things seriously
I would take more chances.
I would take more trips. I would climb more
*   mountains, swim more rivers.*
I would eat more ice cream and less beans. I would
*   perhaps have more actual troubles, but fewer*

imaginary ones.

*You see, I'm one of those people who live seriously
and sanely hour after hour, day after day.*

*Oh, I've had my moments. And if I had to do it
over again I'd have more of them.*

*In fact, I'd try to have nothing else. Just moments,
one after another, instead of living so many years
ahead of each day.*

*I've been one of those persons who never goes
anywhere*

*Without a thermometer, a hot-water bottle, a
raincoat and a parachute.*

*If I had to do it again, I would travel lighter than I
have.*

*If I had to live my life over, I would start barefoot
early in the spring and stay that way later in the
fall.*

I would go to more dances.

I would ride more merry-go-rounds.

I would pick more daisies.

Possessions

Alcoholics, sexaholics, drug or food addicts, anyone who
has not overcome a compulsive behaviour pattern before
death, has grounds for regret far less gentle than had
Nadine Stair. At death they tend to get stuck in a lower
astral plane, or may even become earthbound. (An earthbound soul can also be someone who is either unaware
that he is dead, or refuses to believe that he is. Even a
person who does not want to leave his material possessions behind can become earthbound.) The addicted
personality will be surrounded by what he is addicted to,
without being able to use it. Eventually he will tire of the

situation and move on. Until he does so he will suffer in a form of self-created hell.

An earthbound or lower astral-bound entity can also become a possessive entity. Unable to satiate his desires, he hangs around living people who can, and absorbs some of their pleasure by a kind of mental osmosis. He will give them a psychic nudge to indulge themselves more frequently. The person affected in this way will sense this – for example, in the case of alcohol, as a desire for a drink, which leads to another drink, and then another. The discarnate entity becomes powerful when he realises that he can manipulate a human personality. He will push more, until the living person's compulsive behaviour becomes obsessional. At this point the aura, or electro-magnetic field around the physical personality, weakens and can develop holes – almost like a jersey that wears thin, and then tears. When this happens the discarnate entity can take over the human mind and control it. People who commit crimes and say: 'a voice told me to do it' are usually possessed. When this happens, the living person's behaviour will become very manipulative of people around him, and his eyes change. He literally has someone else using his body. In cases like this, it is important to remember that both the incarnate and discarnate need help.

Once the discarnate entity has been sent on his way – to a plane of healing and learning – the person who is incarnate needs help and support while he adjusts. It is similar to letting the physical body heal after an operation. He also needs to heal his auric field. This can be done standing in the sun and mentally absorbing the sun's rays into the body through the solar plexus. When he feels filled with sunlight, he must imagine or visualise radiating sunlight around him in the form of a bubble. Crystals, colours and sound, to work on the chakras, will all help to rebuild the auric field. I have found that when addictive persons are taught to see auras (which can also be done with Kirlian photography) they get better very quickly. Medicine of the future will encompass a much greater awareness of how we affect our subtle or invisible bodies by what we do to our physical bodies.

Preparation For Birth

Once the personality has completed his life assessment he is guided towards the experiences and teaching which he needs to help him progress.

In the past the time lapse between incarnations was approximately 50 years – unless a person was either the victim or cause of violent death. Today it appears that the break between one physical life and the next is much shorter, with some souls reincarnating almost immediately.

Description of afterlife or in-between life dimensions vary enormously, depending on the evolution of the person who, under hypnosis, is able to see it. People who have been ill for a long time before death appear to rest in places similar to nursing-homes. Some drift about doing very little until impelled to incarnate again. Others are drawn to study further particular subjects that interested them on earth. Those whose interests are strong appear to lead busy in-between lives, and attend schools, classes, and libraries, while others enjoy the atmosphere, and continue an existence similar to their earthly one.

Rudolf Steiner wrote: 'Life between death and a new birth is as rich and varied as is life here between birth and death.'

In-between life planes are really different states of consciousness, so everyone will perceive them in a slightly different way. However, those who have had even the smallest peep into them all describe the love that obliterates all fear and negativity, the sense of timelessness and interconnectedness with all of creation, the brilliant colours and exquisite music, the peace and ecstasy almost impossible to put into words.

Robert Monroe, author of *Journeys out of the Body* and *Far Journeys*, introduced thousands of people to the idea of OBEs (out of body experiences) and excursions into different realms of consciousness. Monroe has seen these planes as a series of inner and outer rings and subrings. He saw that each ring contained a different category of people, who took their place on the ring that matched their stage of evolution.

Monroe also saw from this non-physical reality that planet earth is unique in the opportunities it offers for the development of intelligence and consciousness. He described the earth as a 'compressed learning system' and said that many souls incarnate to experience the limitations of a physical body because it 'engenders concentration of certain energies available only in that state'. We are also meant to develop, control and express our own creative force, which is connected with the prime energy of the universe. Robert Monroe says he saw thousands upon thousands of souls virtually queuing up to await their turn to incarnate. Apparently there are more souls clamouring to enter the earth plane than there are places for them. We need to remember how lucky we are to have our present opportunities and make full use of them instead of vaguely passing through our lives.

Friedrich Nietzsche summed it up neatly in these words from his book *Eternal Recurrence*: 'Let us stamp the impress of eternity upon our lives. Live so that you may desire to live again – that is your duty – for in any case you will live again.'

Creating The Blueprint

Once it is time to plan for the next incarnation – with the help of advisers, who ensure that our lives will contain exactly what we need for our spiritual growth – we create a blueprint for it. This advisory board may consist of highly evolved teachers, guides and guardians, members of our soul-family and even pre-deceased friends and relations. Everything is considered and worked out, from the choice of male or female body, parents and family members, health, education, social and financial status, country and time of birth, political conditions of the time, talents, challenges, future spouse and children, right through to the time and type of death.

If the time of death is pre-planned many of our current life-prolonging techniques such as transplants and life-support machines for the very sick and elderly may be a waste of time. Gildas, the guide and teacher of medium and counsellor Ruth White, said in response to a question concerning organ transplants: 'No man can be made to live longer than the span which has been ordained for him, for though the physical may appear to keep going, the spirit will depart when it is time for departure approaches, so that all the labour, all the clever techniques, all the suffering, are expended for a cause not worth the quality of these things.'

Our pre-incarnation plans are made with complete soul-understanding of the reason for each choice. We should remember this when we are tempted to bemoan our fate – we literally criticise the choices we ourselves made. Most of us forget or resist this idea. (Past life therapy can help us to find our own pre-life blueprint and live it out consciously.) We also spend so much time worrying about how to feed and clothe ourselves, put a roof over our heads, get a job, find a lover and get on with the people around us that we lose sight of the fact that we came to earth to develop spiritual understanding, to enjoy life, not merely to survive.

Instead of thinking of retirement and old age as a time of freedom, relaxation from the pressures of a career, a progressive release from identification with the body and an opportunity to put our spiritual selves in order, we fear it as much as, if not more than, death. Rather than dread old age as a time of winding up a life, we should see it as a time of preparation for a new experience, a new beginning.

Many years ago Seth said: 'I am here to tell you that your joy is not dependent on your youth, for I am hardly young.' He also said: 'I can assure you that death is another beginning, and that when you are dead you are not silenced. For is this, the voice that you hear now, silence? Is the presence that you sense within this room death?'

Old people's homes could give classes in how to leave the body – rather as pre-natal classes teach pregnant women how to give birth. Once people know how to leave the body at will, that consciousness exists whether in or out of the body, they would lose all fear of death. In fact, Robert Monroe has developed a programme called 'Going Home', in which very old or dying patients are helped to go beyond the veil and come back. They then know what to expect when they make their final release, and relax into death happy and fearless. (Address for more information about this programme at back of book.)

Meanwhile, let's think of old age in T. S. Eliot's words:

Old men ought to be explorers.
Here and there does not matter.
We must be still, and still moving
Into another intensity,
For further union, a deeper consciousness . . .
In the end is my beginning.

9

EXPLORING YOUR
OWN PAST LIVES

Time present and time past,
Are both perhaps present in time future,
and time future contained in time past.

T. S. ELIOT, Burnt Norton

My son was 14 years old when he disappeared. We were living in Australia at the time, and the shock nearly killed me. It was like a death without a body to mourn, and I became desperately ill.

Despite the help of my now ex-husband, the police, private detectives and friends, he was never found. Twelve years later he re-appeared, only to vanish again, and I have not seen him since.

The second disappearance was easier to deal with than the first. At the first time an Indian doctor told me that my physical symptoms suggested that I was unconsciously committing a form of suicide, and that I must pull myself together. He prescribed a variety of herbs, acupuncture and body-work to help me do so. During his treatment, which was enormously helpful, I realised that the only person who could help me was me.

Six months after my son's initial disappearance, and while still in a zombie-like state of shock, I walked into the book department of a large store. Suddenly a woman (a complete stranger) walked up to me, put her hands on my shoulder, and said in a Cockney accent: 'You've been through a bloody crucifixion! You and your son had a time to be together, and that time came to an end. It was pre-destined, and part of your future work – is there anything else you want to know?'

In my numbed and shocked state, confused by her appearance and words, I shook my head, said 'No,' and walked away. I later regretted not having questioned her further.

For six months I had prayed, begged, and beseeched God, angels, guides – anyone, whether physical or non-physical – for information about my son. Nothing happened! I felt betrayed, especially because information about other missing or murdered children poured into my mind with ease. I now realised that my own shock and despair created around me an almost impenetrable, emotional fog, and that this woman's physical touch on my shoulder helped to break through it.

I went home and asked through prayer and meditation for more insight into what this woman had told me. Immediately, and as clearly as if a human voice spoke in my ear, I heard the words: 'Unless you accept what has happened without resistance, you will never find the answers you seek.' I replied: 'Help me to do this – it is almost impossible.' The voice said: 'You chose it. Now you must deal with it.'

Depressed by this answer I lay back, closed my eyes, and suddenly (and spontaneously) regressed into a past-life memory. I saw myself as an Atlantean priestess, chosen – with others because of our psychic abilities – to give birth to babies who were meant to embody the thoughts we were trained to put into them. I saw that many babies born were malformed, and as a result misused. I began to speak out against this experimental practice, in public as well as to my son. As punishment, when my son was six years old, he was taken from me and I never saw him again. I died in prison. My emotional refusal to release him, to let him go at that time, set in motion my need to do so again in this life. It was a form of sacrifice. I then saw a life in which I had been arrogant, intolerant of people less intelligent or less fortunate than myself. I ignored their suffering, and became obsessed with beauty and material possessions. I loved to dress up in silk, satin and velvet (I still do!) and had three or four lovers at once. I mocked a servant who begged me to take her illegitimate son into my household. My refusal to do so caused him to be sold as a slave, and she never saw him again.

As well as many very ordinary lives such as those of beggars, street-cleaners, chimney sweeps, builders of the Great Wall of China and the pyramids, I saw myself as a wily horse-and-camel trader, galloping across vast stretches of Arabian desert; a manipulative Chinese courtesan; a pious nun; a carefree Spanish gypsy; a rebellious young monk in a Tibetan lamasery (rebellious because my family had placed me there in an attempt to 'buy themselves good Karma') as well as a life in which I abandoned my wife and family in order to go to war. My motivation was self-glorification, rather than to protect my family, tribe or country, and they never recovered from what seemed to them a betrayal.

In my present life I was six years old when my father vanished from my life. For forty years I did not know if he was dead or alive. My spontaneous past-life review not only showed me he was my child in that other time, but also put me in touch with the reason for many of my present-day traumas, relationships and health problems, and enabled me to get on with my life again.

If past-life recall can help *me* overcome what seemed at the time to be insurmountable problems, then it will also be able to help you, the reader of this book.

Motivation For Exploring Past Lives

Dr J B Rhine, director of Parapsychology at Duke University USA, said: 'The psychology of today looks at the mind of today. The psychology of tomorrow will look at the past.' This is what regression or past-life therapy is all about.

This is neither mystical nor difficult, and we can do it ourselves – although if no inner work has been done before it is better to start off with an experienced psychotherapist or guide.

Ideally, this should be a person we both like and trust. Someone who is willing to help us review and heal the memories of *this* life, as well as those of the past – including childhood, birth, in the womb, conception and pre-conception. He should also help us find our own memories of other lives, with us making the major effort, rather than announce to us whom he perceives or imagines we were.

Whether we do it ourselves or use a guide, past-life therapy works best when we have a valid reason for going back. Mere curiosity may provide the original stimulus, but real *need* provides the authentic motive – for example, to understand and forgive parents, release repressed emotion or blocks, recognize *why* the people around us are the way they are, discover a health or relationship problem, find and develop talents, (which may be part of our life/soul purpose), understand that addiction (to anything) is a form of emotional suppression and that chronic patterns of self-hate and self-criticism raise stress and weaken our immune system, and can be healed by unravelling the original cause.

During A Regression Session

Although this has never happened to me, it is possible during a regression spontaneously to speak in a foreign language never spoken nor understood before. The term for this is Xenoglossy. Glossolalia, which describes a form of speaking in tongues, can also occur, but rarely does. Glossolalia sounds a little like a language, but is incomprehensible, and emerges more like a stream of sound.

Cryptomnesia is another word that crops up between regression therapists and their patients – as well as those who are anti the idea of reincarnation. This means that the past-life memories which surface, and appear to be totally genuine, are based on a novel read, a film seen, a story overheard, which are so completely absorbed into the subconscious and unconscious that they are identified as one's own. Cryptomnesia is a form of false or pseudo-recall, but has a totally different energy to true past-life memory. An experienced therapist can pick this up, and redirect the patient towards his own truth.

Hypnagogic images (the pictures, faces and scenes which can appear in our mind's eye as we relax) can also be the first stage of attuning to the memory of other lives. These images can be as clear as if we were watching television, and it is important to let them come and go without judgement or attachment.

Hypnagogic images also flow into our mind's eye when we begin to fall asleep or wake up. Deep relaxation, which is a vital part of past-life therapy, slows our brain-wave rhythm from Beta into Alpha and then Theta. The merge between Alpha and Theta is where dreaming begins continues with greater impact in deep Theta. This slow brain-wave rhythm is where we can regress into ancient memories of this and other lives.

In 1980 I attended a lecture given by Dr Peter Fenwick, a consultant neurophysiologist at St Thomas' Hospital, London, on the neurophysiology of the brain. In it he said that, not only do the 90-minute cycles of right and left brain activity, which stimulate sleep and dreaming, occur at night, but also throughout the day.

Thus during the day our thinking and behaviour is also influenced by which brain hemisphere is activated. We move from 90-minutes of left-brain logical, linear thinking into 90 minutes where imagination, emotion and intuition dominate. In other words, if I take an exam in mathematics or geometry when I am in my emotional, intuitive phase I am going to find it far more difficult to pass than if I were in my logical, analytical mode. By contrast, if I want to meditate, use my imagination or my inner senses, it will not work so well if at that time my brain activity is logical and linear.

I was struck by the idea that if we could assess at which time of the day we moved into left or right brain thinking, we could make life much easier for ourselves by doing what comes most naturally at that particular time of the day. This of course applies to past-life therapy too. Find the time when we are most intuitive, receptive, imaginative and right-brained, and we are far more likely to discover memories of other lives.

It may be helpful to know that, according to Dr Fenwick, there is considerable data available about the 24-hour cycle in man. Apparently we are at our lowest ebb at 2 am, become slowly alert through early and later morning, until we are at our first peak at 12 noon. We then dip until 3 pm, revive to reach our second peak around 9 pm, and the decline again until 2 am. (I personally find that I wake, alert and active, around 3 am – at which time I can get my best work done – and by 9 pm I am so dissolved that it is all I can do to crawl into bed. However, Dr Fenwick gave this lecture 15 years ago, and our whole concept of time has changed since then.)

A past-life therapist will initially guide his subject into a state of deep relaxation before asking questions that stimulate past-life recall. He may also use hypnosis, or induce a mild trance (which is virtually the same thing) in order to lift his subject's mind away from ordinary everyday living into a level of consciousness in which he can overview the patterns of this and other lives. (This is similar to the difference between seeing life from within a car driven along a local high street, to covering the same route in a helicopter, when all manner of things hidden from the limited vision below now become clearly visible.)

One life or several can be reviewed in the same session, dependent on what comes up with each individual. One of my clients discovered a life in which he was similar in personality to Hitler. In fact initially we both thought that he was indeed the reincarnation of Hitler. It took hours to work through every facet of that life, and help him to assimilate that information so that it was healing and helpful rather than destructive to his present life. (Remember that no matter if we were baddies or goodies, it was all necessary as part of our journey towards self-realisation.)

Another session might enable a person to get in touch with eight or nine lives, although it is better not to try for too many at once. In America some years ago I worked with a wonderful healer called Kay Ortmans, who developed a special massage called Wellsprings as a means to help her patients regress. During one six-hour session with Kay 80 past-life personalities popped up – at which point we decided that enough was enough and stopped!

(This session was in part a training for some of her students, an opportunity for them to see how Wellsprings worked, and what the results could be. I do not recommend that you should attempt to see so many lives in so short a space of time.)

Sometimes a regression subject will fear he is making up the characters and scenes that start flowing into his mind. 'It cannot be real. It's only my imagination making up some silly story.' The difference between a real or fantasy image is the depth of emotion, the mental and physical reaction to what is seen when the memories begin to surface, contrasted with the absence of these in a fantasy. The emotions and sensations that come up with genuine recall are as vivid as though they were part of the present. As past-life therapy is a way of re-living the past, this should not be surprising. Also, a fantasy can be changed at will, while a true image will not go away.

Sometimes a person will fear too what he may discover about himself. In my own life and in my own work I have found that no memory will reveal itself until or unless the time is right. There appears to be an inbuilt safety-mechanism in our consciousness which protects us from knowing too much before we are able to deal with, and use, the knowledge to improve the quality of this present life. We can also say a prayer in which we ask that only what we need for our highest or soul good be brought into our awareness. As I mentioned in Chapter 5, I always say a prayer before and after my own sessions. I ask that only that which is of God, good, love and truth be present, that anything inappropriate to the consciousness of X. . .Y. . . or Z at this time may be transformed, and I invoke the presence of the patient's own angels, guides and teachers. I end my session with a prayer of thanks, on behalf of myself and my patient.

During regression one person may see, with his inner

sight, as clearly as if he watched a film or television programme unfold in front of him. His body may respond by physically re-enacting the part he watches himself play, while at the same time he can feel hot, cold, shivery or even nauseous. Another person may sense past lives through feeling, shapes, symbols, colours or sounds. These can be used as keys to an in-depth and more understandable experience. All are produced by the imagination, which is the greatest key of all if and when we want to explore the invisible depths of different levels of our own consciousness.

Occasionally a person will see nothing but blackness, pink dots, or a blob of one colour. To see deep purple/violet or blue/indigo indicates that we're in touch with our own Akashic records and a higher level of consciousness. (These colours are also the most commonly seen during meditation.) We can merge with the colour and simply ask ourselves, or let the therapist ask, questions. If we let the answers pop up spontaneously, 'by themselves', rather than working them out logically, we can still get great insight and self-knowledge, even if no pictures appear.

Others review lives from the sense of being completely inside a past-life personality. This person's inner senses seem as physically alive as his outer senses. He can taste, feel, smell, touch and hear everything his inner eye reveals, as if it were happening at that very moment. One of my patients smelled the fragrance of baking bread so clearly that she sat up and suggested that I should turn my oven off before the bread burnt. Another could barely move inside the heavy rough-textured monk's robe she sensed herself to be wearing. At the same time, she was perfectly aware of lying on my bed, clad in shorts and a T-shirt.

Love, Relationships And Past Lives

During regression we can sometimes be almost overwhelmed by feelings of nostalgia. This is especially true for the person who begins to unravel threads that connect this life's loves to those of the past. Many of my patients are in tears when they re-experience a love lost, forgotten, or misunderstood at the time – especially when they compare their feelings then with those of the present.

Today much of what we call love is based on lack of self-love and self-acceptance, the need for someone else to prop us up and make us happy, the obsessive desire for a man or woman who rejects us, fear of abandonment, loneliness, or even guilt.

Past-life therapy shows that we often subconsciously seek a partner who reminds us of a past-life identity – our own or their's. We are drawn to people who express qualities we ourselves have denied. Examples are the introvert drawn to the extrovert, and vice versa. Sometimes we develop a relationship with a person who was an enemy in the past. Drawn together by a vague sense of recognition (sometimes combined with foreboding) we move into a relationship-dance of love and hate. (The opposite of love is not hate, but indifference. To hate, one has to care. Hate is misunderstood love.) This usually results in constant battles between the couple, combined with an inability to separate. Instead of feeling sorry for their situation, we should respect this present relationship as an opportunity for them to work out old Karma.

Most love partners are projections of what we perceive at the moment to be the perfect man or woman, (usually subsequently impossible to live with) as well as what we refuse to see or acknowledge in ourselves. Our problems, blocks, failings and misgivings are reflected back to us in a sort of mirror-image. Instead of recognising this as helpful, we usually blame each other for not being the person each wants the other to be.

For example Jenny, a successful barrister, married Michael, an equally successful television producer. Jenny expected Michael to share the household chores, including preparation of the occasional meal, helping with the shopping, laundry and watering the garden. To Jenny's fury, especially when they both returned from a hard day's work, Michael sat and watched TV, or read a newspaper, expecting Jenny to fall into his stereotype vision of 'wife waits hand and foot on husband', Jenny tried everything, from asking Michael for help, refusing to cook or clean herself, to staying out late at night with friends. She also cried, cajoled and sulked, all to no avail. Whatever she said or did had no effect.

Finally a friend suggested regression therapy. Jenny then discovered a life in which she had been a demanding lady of the manor/mistress of the house, and Michael her servant. She kept him busy from morning till night – often with tasks that were totally unnecessary. She suddenly saw that, before incarnation in this life, Michael chose to be served rather than to be a servant. Who better to serve him than his former employer? Because she now under-stood why Michael was the way he was, Jenny dropped her demands for help. A few days later Michael began, unasked, to help with many of the chores he had previously ignored. Jenny discovered a universal truth, that when we let go of what we think we want another person to be or do, we free him to be himself, which is often what we wanted him to be in the first place. The demand that a person be or not be a certain way creates a barrier of resistance that blocks the previous possibility of it happening.

In another relationship, described during a seminar

given by Raymond Moody, a psychiatrist and author of many books on near-death experience and reincarnation, a couple, after many years of happy sex, ran into difficulties. The wife refused her husband's sexual advances and, during therapy, accused him of sexual abuse and domination. Her husband retaliated by saying that his wife had been a willing participant. During regression they discovered a life in which he, as a knight, sexually used and abused a servant girl (now the wife) in his castle. He subsequently betrayed her by trying to pass her on to one of his friends. When Moody questioned this couple further, he discovered that their initial this-life sexual activity had been enjoyable and uninhibited. After some years, the husband suggested that they swap partners with other couples. The wife was devastated, and lost all interest in sex. It triggered her unconscious past-life memory of creeping into her then lover's chamber and, instead of finding him, being faced with one of his friends who said: 'Don't be afraid! I can give you as much fun as he does.' These discoveries enabled them to re-establish their relationship. They now understood where some of their fears and tendencies originated, and accepted that their this-life partnership was a means to heal the past.

Once we accept that present relationships are opportunities to work out past-life Karma, no matter whether good, bad or indifferent, life changes dramatically. Past-life therapy helps us to see that to make another person responsible for our happiness is to court disaster. We *must* take responsibility for ourselves. Instead of looking outside for another person to fulfil our needs, we must look within. When we are whole and secure within ourselves we stop projecting our own imbalance on the people around us.

Paul Brunton wrote: 'There is a way that leads neither to the East nor to the West: it is entirely inwards, and if you follow this mysterious track, inevitably your outer life will begin to change its own face.'

To mediate, visualize, listen to our intuition, act on our inner feelings, use past-life or regression therapy to heal the past, is to follow that inward track.

Before describing some of the myriad and most successful (in my experience) ways of doing this, I would like to give a brief overview of other disciplines that can both trigger and/or confirm the truth of a past-life memory.

Other Disciplines Useful In Past-Life Exploration

Astrology
One of the most popular and best known is astrology, which can given insight into other lives, and is based on the relationship between the position of the planets, the signs, and the time and place of a person's birth. Astrology provides a map of consciousness in which we can see our strengths, weaknesses and Karmic patterns. The first house, Aries, provides lessons of personality – who I am. The second, Taurus, is to do with 'what I have', especially in the area of money, possessions and resources. The third, Gemini, is about communication and thought. Cancer, number four, concerns family, home and feelings. The fifth, Leo is all about will (usually wilful rather than willing) and creativity. The sixth, Virgo, is connected to health and analytic assessment. (Virgos at their worst can be too perfectionistic – at their best they can cut through the rubbish of other people's false ideas.) The seventh, Libra, is about balance and partnership. The eighth, Scorpio (dreaded by most other signs – I know, because I am a triple Scorpio) symbolises death, regeneration and

sexuality. Sagittarius, the ninth house, reflects aspiration to higher consciousness. Capricorn, in the tenth house, is to do with career and achievement, the use of both past and present abilities. Aquarius, or the eleventh house, is concerned with friendships, people, and how to serve humanity. Pisces, in the twelfth house, is a sign of the hidden, the mystic, who can often get into trouble by swimming in different directions – feelings conflict with the mind. The challenge here is to integrate all other signs.

The I Ching

The *I Ching*, or *Book of Change,* is an ancient Chinese system of self-analysis which portrays every possible circumstance and cycle of life that we may experience. It shows the interaction between Yang (masculine energy) and Yin (feminine energy). According to R L Wing, who wrote the *I Ching Workbook*, the *I Ching* may be the oldest book on the planet. In Wing's words: 'The early authors of *I Ching* observed the stars and tides, the plants and animals, and the cycles of all natural events. At the same time, they observed the patterns of relationships in families and societies, the practice of business, the craft of government, the grim art of warfare, the eternal human drama of love, ambition, conflict and honour. They made no attempt to create a fixed chart of the cosmos. Instead they organically grew a guide to the way things change.'

To use the *I Ching* for divination of past, present or future, we must drop yarrow sticks or coins onto a flat surface six times, and interpret their Yin-Yang balance. (These interpretations are clearly laid out in the *I Ching*.) In Wing's words: 'This is a way of stopping the world or time – like clicking the shutter of a camera in order to capture the picture of the moment.' It must be done with a particular question in mind as a way of aligning oneself and one's circumstances within the background of what is unfolding in the universe. Lao Tzu, Confucius, Chang Tzu and, even more recently, Richard Wilhelm and Carl Jung, were all fascinated by the accuracy of the *I Ching's* responses to the questions they put to it. Confucius believed in using the book 'as a credo to develop, determine and define his inner development.' The *I Ching* consists of 64 hexagrams, all of which represent phases of human experience. We can use it to discover past, present and future lives.

The Tarot

The tarot consists of a deck of 78 cards which symbolically portray life. Each card depicts a life experience. The 22 major Arkana (arcane means hidden or secret esoteric teaching) represent the psychological and emotional changes we go through from self to divine or cosmic awareness. The 40 minor Arkana – from which our playing cards came – depict our environment, and how each area affects us. For example, pentacles or coins mean money and energy. How do we use or waste it? How do we handle our resources, energy or time? Wands are to do with action, work, business; cups with affairs of the heart, emotion, romance and love. Swords represent the mind, and often depict frustration, resistance and mental struggle with the circumstances of life. There are also 16 Court cards – kings, queens, pages and knights – which represent the people in our lives.

There are over a 100 different types of tarot originating from the hieroglyphs inscribed on the walls of the pyramids and the underground chambers leading from the pyramids to the Sphynx. Students spent time there meditating on each symbol until they understood its meaning. It was part of their training to become an adept in a temple or esoteric school.

The Cabbala

The Cabbala, the esoteric tradition of the Hebrew religion, is another way to decipher the transition from physical to spiritual consciousness. The Cabbala depicts the tree of life with 22 paths connecting to spheres which represent avenues of growth between different levels of consciousness. The paths of the Cabbala are linked to the 22 letters of the Hebrew alphabet. They show the different energies we use during our process of involution and evolution.

Numerology

Another system to help us define and make the most opportunity of our life's experience is numerology. Pythagoras believed that divine laws are reflected in the mathematics of numbers. The Chinese believed that odd numbers were Yang or masculine, and the even numbers Yin or feminine.

Basic numerology suggests that A = 1, B = 2, C = 3 and so forth. There are many excellent books on numerology which can help us understand that no numbers come into our life by accident – including car registration and telephone numbers. Numerical interpretations of our name, date and place of birth can give us amazing insight into why we incarnate and what we are here to do.

Acupuncture, Crystals and Other Methods

Hand, aura, tea-leaf, coffee-grain and crystal-ball readings, kinesiology (or Touch for Health), the metamorphic technique, reflexology, psychometry and acupuncture can all help us discover who we were in the past and how our past is affecting our present. To practise these techniques ourselves, rather than to go to someone else for a reading, not only opens doors into our subconscious, but also develops our intuitive/psychic sensitivity.

Shirley MacLaine used acupuncture to stimulate her own past-life recall. Raymond Moody has had such success at crystal-ball gazing (known as 'scrying') that he now teaches his students how to do it.

The crystal ball is used as a point of focus for the gazer, and is best done in candlelight, with a dark cloth under the ball to prevent outside images being reflected in it. Taking time to stare at and into the ball lowers the brainwave rhythm into Alpha, so that we begin to see with the inner eye rather than the outer. Initially images may come from this-life, for example scenes from childhood or particularly memorable events. If we persevere, especially if we have a firm question in mind concerning the past, the pictures change and develop. Six (or more) people may stare into a crystal-ball at once, and get totally different images. This is because what comes up is a projection into the crystal of what each viewers' subconscious and unconscious want them to see.

We can follow the same method using a mirror, a bowl of water, or an ordinary crystal. (In other words, a crystal not shaped and polished into a ball.) Window crystals are particularly effective for this, and can be recognized by a large diamond-shaped facet (or window) in the centre. If we gaze into this window – or even hold it to the centre of our forehead – (the third eye chakra) – it will show us pictures in the same way as the crystal-ball does. Another stone I have found to be very effective in triggering past-life recall is sugalite, also known as luvulite. Sugalite balances the pineal and pituitary glands and stimulates third eye or inner vision seeing. To meditate on a ruby opens up our seed atom connection (contained within the heart) to God, and can activate the memory of our own Akashic records. If a ruby is out of your price range – although there are many small/uncut/unpolished rubies available at little cost – *imagine* a ruby or red rose in the heart. Concentrate on this image until the heart appears to become liquid fire, and then begin to ask for the past-life information you require.

Dreams

Dreams are yet another source of knowledge and inspiration which can be used to tap into past-life memory. A dream, like meditation, provides a link between inner and outer worlds, and puts us in touch with a wisdom far greater than that of our normal waking selves. Dreams introduce us to the huge cast of characters living inside us, and constantly comment on what we are doing with our lives. Because a dream is a psychic reading from and about our own personal Akashic record, we can ask dreams for insight and information about past, present and future lives.

Mary asked a dream for information concerning a colleague with whom she had much conflict. (To do this, write down on a piece of paper or pad: 'I want to dream – I want to remember my dream', followed by the question you want answered. To ask questions of a dream is called 'dream incubation', an ancient art practised for aeons of time, especially in the area of health and healing.) Mary had three dreams in which she saw herself and her male colleague, almost as if watching a Walt Disney cartoon, as archeologists in Egypt digging for artefacts around the pyramids, then earlier as Egyptian priests burying the very same artefacts for which they sought in their later life. She also saw herself and her male colleague even further back, as overseers of the building of some of the pyramids. In each life, there was conflict, turmoil and competition. Mary's realisation that the sales team, of which the two of them were now both a part, was another kind of pyramid-building, made her able to laugh about the situation, rather than feel resentment. As a result, she dropped her competitive edge, and, after a time, so did he.

Past-life memories, no matter how they come, help us to let go of emotional traumas. When we realise the impermanence of life – as well as its importance – we can, and should, have a sense of humour about it.

Drawing

To draw is another powerful means of becoming aware of our feelings, our inner self and our past – especially when the drawings are done within a circle or mandala. Jung wrote that the basic motive of the mandala 'is the premonition of a centre of personality, a kind of central point within the psyche, to which everything is related, by which everything is arranged, and which itself is a source of energy.' Long before I read these words, I began to draw huge circles on the floor – I actually sat inside the circles and drew around myself – using newspaper, brown wrapping paper, or vast sheets from advertising pads. I found myself literally 'sucked into' what I drew, like falling through the hole of a long-playing gramaphone record. I saw past, present and future entwined and co-existent, and also how my present reality affected my past and future realities.

Listening with an Open Mind

There is no end to how we may get in touch with anything we need to know. The secrets of the universe, as well as our own personal records, are written into everything we see around us. The skies, stars, cloud patterns, trees, stones, hills and mountains, sacred sites, crystals, pyramids and crystal skulls, are brimful of information for anyone willing to see and listen with an open mind and heart.

An example of what can happen if we listen with an open mind is the story of my French friend Henri. Henri's life fell apart, his marriage broke up, his children and his home were taken away from him. Almost suicidal, he slumped under a tree in a nearby wood, and wondered what to do. After 30 or 40 minutes Henri, who was not at all 'into this kind of thing' at the time, thought that the tree spoke to him. According to Henri, the tree said: 'It's all very well for you to feel sorry for yourself, but I've got a bloody great nail piercing that root (*un maudit clou percant ma racine à la gauche*) the one you've got your foot on. What's more, it's been there for more than 100 years.' Bemused and thinking his own traumas had made him slightly crazy, Henri began to scrabble around in the earth that lay around the root. Sure enough, he found an enormous nail piercing the root of the tree against which he sat. Henri removed it and, according to him, 'The tree appeared to give a sigh of relief.' Since then Henri has used the tree as a means of communication with his own teachers, guides and Akashic records. He leans against the tree, sometimes posing aloud the questions he has and sometimes silently, in his mind. After a short time the answers float back to him.

Journeying Powerful
Paths To The Inner Source

All the disciplines I have mentioned, and of course there are many more, allow us to gain access to both higher and lower levels of consciousness. I believe that originally man was meant to let his higher or super self direct his normal or ordinary self. Today modern man lets his lower – or sub and unconscious selves – direct his conscious behaviour. (In other words, he *reacts* from emotion rather than *acts* from will and ignores the superior intelligence of the higher self.) As we move towards the end of this century, we are pushed in numerous ways to change this. In order to survive and be happy we must look within for the intelligent soul-connected part of our mind that can give us the direction we need.

The Mind

For me, meditation, visualisation and imagination are the most powerful paths to that inner source. Imagination is the channel between the conscious, subconscious and unconscious. It converts the invisible into the visible, creating images for us to see and understand, translating information from lower and higher selves to our conscious waking selves. During the day this is felt rather than seen, in the form of moods, feelings, flashes of intuition and sometimes through daydreams and fantasies. At night imagination brings the same information to us in the form of dreams.

Hermann Hesse wrote in *Siddartha*: 'During meditation it is possible to dispel time, to see simultaneously all the past, present and future, and then everything is Brahman. Therefore it seems to me that everything that exists is good – death as well as life, sin as well as holiness, wisdom as well as folly.'

So how do we ordinary mortals put ourselves in such a state? Edgar Cayce said: 'Began with that in hand, but begin if there would be anything accomplished. Talk is well, action is wise, deeds are golden.'

To 'begin with that in hand' – from the point of triggering past-life recall – might be to travel to a foreign country, looking at a world map to decide on the areas and languages we are most drawn to, or repulsed by. (Even without a map we can do the same thing.) Or we can choose a certain period in history that, again, we feel a connection or resistance to. Books on a library shelf can stimulate memories of the past. So can pictures in an art gallery, and films at the cinema or on TV. However, the most immediate tools we have to hand are those of mind and body.

The Body

To encourage the imaginative part of our mind to co-operate with, rather than fight against, us we should first put our physical bodies in order. A healthy diet, adequate sleep and exercise, deep breathing, massage, movement to music (or dance) long soaks in the sea or warm baths, can all help the body, and thus the mind, to relax.

The Alexander technique, aromatherapy, aura-soma (a system of vibrational colour-healing) and yoga, are all excellent ways of making us more body conscious.

The Alexander technique is a method of understanding how the body is naturally designed to work. It involves a re-education of how to use the body in such a way that our own psycho-equilibrium can be restored, so that we have heightened awareness of ourselves and the world around us, as well as many other levels of consciousness. Aromatherapy is basically massage with fragrant, herbal oils. These are usually chosen by the aromatherapist who is trained intuitively to select the herbs most beneficial to us at any one time. Aura-soma is self-selective colour healing. In other words you choose the colours you are most drawn to, which are then interpreted by a qualified practitioner. They can be used for massage, aura healing and meditation. (Violet dabbed on the throat or third eye can stimulate past-life memory, orange over violet can help us deal with Karma, while orange on its' own is a shock-absorber and can stabilise or ground us if we suffer an accident or a particularly traumatic regression.)

Yoga is considered by the uninitiated to be an almost violent form of exercise in which one has to contort one's body into unimaginable positions. Before I met English yoga teacher Enid Gulf, I resisted any form of yoga as I felt incapable of putting my head between my legs and then under left or right armpit all at the same time. Thanks to her I now realise that basic yoga includes body stretching, shaking and slapping and is not confined to standing on one's head with one's right ankle round one's left ear.

Yoga, aura-soma, aromatherapy and the Alexander technique are designed for long-term rather than one-off sessions (which does not mean we cannot benefit from an introduction to any of them.)

Relaxing the Mind and Body

Meanwhile any form of inner meditative journey works better if we physically relax immediately beforehand. This may mean taking a few moments to stretch and bend while inhaling and exhaling as deeply as possible. Breathe in through the nose, hold the breath as long as possible, and exhale through the mouth, deeply and firmly as if blowing out a candle. Another simple exercise is to lie on the floor and imagine breathing out tension little by little from each part of the body – it does not matter if we start from the head or the toe. Having established a rhythm of conscious breathing we should then concentrate on each muscle, limb and organ of the body. Tense and tighten the left foot and leg, then the right, followed by the stomach, buttocks, arms, shoulders, chest, back, neck and face until, although we are aware of our bodies, at the same time we are no longer inside them. (For people who hate the idea of any kind of exercise no matter how small, I suggest they simply visualise themselves doing it.) In my own sessions I then guide my patient to imagine sunlight or colour filling every cell, muscle and tissue with love, health and vitality from top to toe before I guide him inwards. For some, this is easier to do by listening to a tape. There are many excellent relaxation tapes available, or we can make one ourselves.

To journey inwards is to start a conversation with a part of ourselves that most of us have forgotten exists. It is our connection with what Jung called the 'collective unconscious', Cayce the 'river of thought', and Paul Solomon named as his 'source'. It is a little like talking to an elder brother, sister, teacher or guide – someone who knows more than we do, but totally understands us at the same time. A child will often interrupt a conversation to draw attention to himself: 'I want a drink of water . . . I'm hungry . . . I want to go to the bathroom . . .' Both body and mind tend to behave like spoiled children when we want to converse with our inner selves. The mind goes off at a tangent, and thinks of hundreds of other things it would (or should) rather do, while the body cramps, twitches and itches. To take time to mentally and physically relax is like giving a spoiled child an orange juice and a box of crayons before talking with a friend. Occupied and happy, he lets us get on with our conversation uninterrupted.

To assist the brain as well as the body to relax, I find it helpful to count backwards slowly from 21 to 0, breathing deeply as I do so. Although some therapists prefer to do this the other way round, ie 0 to 21 (or any other number chosen in the moment), for me going backwards works better.

Other ways to relax the mind – which means to slow the brainwave rhythm from Beta into Alpha – are to listen to music, daydream, reflect on happy memories (a special holiday, person or event).

Imagine a stroll through a wood, along a beach, a mountain-climb, or lazing in thick green grass bathed in the warmth of the sun. The more we can mentally, imaginatively conjure up the sights, scents and sounds of nature, the more effective this type of exercise will be. Hear the birdsong, the rustle of leaves in a tree, the splash and trickle of water in a pool or in a stream, trail a hand or a foot in the water and feel its coolness against the skin, or trickle a few drops into the mouth and savour the taste, see the scuffle of rabbits in the grass, the brilliant splashes of red, blue and white from wild poppies, scabius or daisies scattered along the path. We can all remember how we felt outside on a beautiful day. We can use these memories to stimulate our inner senses to re-create the same atmosphere.

To take even five minutes to do this kind of exercise before any kind of inner work is similar to setting a scene on a stage before the curtain goes up. It creates a backdrop against which the play more easily unfolds.

Regressing To A Past Life

Although I have found it more effective to imagine myself going down and back when I want to explore my sub and unconscious, and to float up and out when I want to contact my higher or superconscious, in my workshops and sessions I use a combination of both.

For example, once my patient (in this book I use 'patient' just as a word, not because I think a person is sick) seems well and truly relaxed, I may guide him in the following way – although of course there are many variations. I speak slowly, leaving spaces between my words, so that he can easily follow the guidance:

'Breathe slowly . . . and deeply . . . and imagine bringing your life force (or physical consciousness) from your toes into your feet . . . then your ankles. Imagine with every breath you take that your life force is lifting up and up, through your legs . . . calves . . . shins . . . knees and thighs

. . with each breath you are more and more relaxed . . .
now . . . slowly . . . easily . . . bringing your life-force up
through the thighs . . . pelvis . . . buttocks . . . up towards
the waist . . . continue to imagine bringing this life-force
up through the chest and back . . . the spine . . . from the
tips of your fingers into the palms of your hands . . . your
wrists, forearms . . . upper arms . . . lifting your
consciousness and attention right away from the lower
part of your body until it seems focused on the neck . . .
then the jaw . . . and cheeks. Breathe it up and up . . . until
it is around your ears . . . eyes . . . back of your head . . .
and rests there for a moment . . . a ball . . . a bubble of
consciousness . . . floating, drifting easily . . . gently . . .
filled with peace . . . until this ball or bubble of
consciousness . . . gently . . . easily begins to float away –
like a balloon . . . lifting higher . . . and higher . . . drifting
through time and space . . . planes and levels of being . . .
higher . . . higher . . . until you gradually feel yourself
returning to a time and a place before this . . . a place of
joy . . . love . . . laughter . . . healing . . . wholeness . . . a
place where you sense a oneness with all of life and all of
creation . . . and . . . as you remember this place,
remember also the presence of your own teacher . . .
mentor . . . or guide . . . someone whose only purpose is
the care and expansion of your own soul . . . allow this
presence to become very clear in your mind . . . in your
imagination . . . even if you see nothing, you will sense
. . . maybe a male . . . or a female . . . a mixture of both
. . . or even a child . . . you may want to reach out for his
. . . or her . . . hand . . . simply sense the love flowing to
you . . . and know this presence is *always* available to help
you with any problems you may have . . . with any
questions you may need answered . . .'

I then suggest that my patient goes with his teacher into
a temple, church, chapel, cathedral, hall, library,

sanctuary or small room (preferably somewhere that represents a sacred space) – a place in or through which he can find the Hall of Records and attune to his own personal Akasha. Sometimes I guide him to seek or ask for his book of life, sometimes I ask that the teacher brings into his awareness the memory of the life most important for him to see at this time. This might be the life immediately prior to his present one, or a life that for some reason most affects this one, the best and worst lives (from the viewpoint of what was done both by and to him), lives in which he previously knew his mother, father, husband, wife, children or friends, was another colour, sex, race or religion, primitive, civilised, a life where a this-life problem began – and so on. Much of my initial suggestion as a key into the life or lives most valuable for him to see in this moment depends on what we have discussed earlier in the session. I then guide him to go back into the memory of the life in question, by suggesting that he let his mind and imagination drift downwards . . . 'back and back . . . deeper and deeper into the memory of this other life . . . this other time . . . until your feet gradually come to rest on solid ground . . . take a moment to sense the ground under your feet . . . is it grass? . . . earth? . . . sand? . . . carpet? . . . pavement?. . . stones? . . . Is it light? . . . dark? . . . inside? . . . outside? . . . Be very aware of your feet . . . are they bare? . . . or do you have shoes on? . . .'

I guide him to imagine and describe the rest of his body . . . big? . . . small? . . . male? . . . female? . . . age? . . . with short or long hair? . . . what type of clothes? . . . what sense of historical era does he have? . . . In what geographical location? Is he alone or with other people? Does life seem easy or difficult? What are the major feelings that come to him with this memory? Is anyone from that life part of his present life, and if so who is this person today? – and so on until we have covered the life as extensively as possible. This includes dealing with forgiveness if necessary, completing anything unfinished as well as looking at death. 'How did that life end? . . . accident? . . . illness? . . . violence? . . . Was it sudden or slow? . . . How did you feel? . . . relieved? . . . sorry? . . . What did you accomplish in that life? . . . What was left undone? . . . What were the major lessons you learned that affect the decisions you make about your next or future lives? . . .' I then guide my patient to lift out of the memory of that life and go back to the place of rest in-between lives where his teacher waits to greet him.

Here we shall look for and assess his present life purpose. This can be done by asking his teacher to tell him, or by looking for the answer in his book of life, or by meeting the council of advisers who helped him to create his life plan. (Remember that soul purpose is recon-nection with God – each life purpose is how we go about it.) At this point he may also choose to look at an in-between-life experience, co-existant or future selves (who might also give him helpful advice), or take an imaginary step into the future to feel for himself what may lie in store. (NB This can be the future of five, 50 or 150 years hence. It does not matter, and still works.) Because the soul sends down aspects of itself on different rays, my patient might choose to ask his soul to reveal these alternate-ray personalities in order to get an overview of the totality of which he is a part. Only when his soul has integrated the experiences of all the rays does a person-ality physically embody the sum total of all his parts. This usually occurs when he is ready for his last incarnation – which may account for personalities such as Mozart and Leonardo da Vinci, who were born with what could be described as the genius and talent of the gods.

To complete a session I guide my patient to integrate the

past personalities he discovered himself to have been, to release those of other people who may unconsciously have impinged on his present life and to thank his teacher and helpers. I then guide his consciousness back to earth and into his body.

To do this yourself, simply imagine the same bubble or balloon of consciousness, or life-force, drifting slowly and easily down until it rests on the top of the head, ready to then be absorbed back into the body. Breathe it into the head, face, shoulders, into and through every cell, muscle, tissue and organ, until it is anchored in the feet. I give my patient time to reorient himself, and when he is ready to open his eyes I ask him to yawn, stretch, sigh, and press his feet to the floor, to affirm his re-connection to the earth and physical reality. He may still feel slightly light-headed, but this ensures that he really is back, and ready to get on with his life again.

Alternative Methods Of Regression

When I use this kind of format, I have never had a patient who was unable to discover one or more relevant lives. However, for the person who prefers either to fly less high, or not to move out of his body, another effective visualisation exercise is the 'Seven Terrace' meditation development by Paul Solomon. We need to start with a garden or meadow as before, but now imagine it round the foot of a mountain. This mountain consists of seven terraced gardens, each one a different colour. The first is red, the second orange, the third yellow, the fourth green, the fifth blue, the sixth violet-purple and the seventh white. (For this exercise, Paul took poetic licence to leave out indigo.) We should leave the meadow and begin slowly to climb the mountain, following a path that winds through the gardens until, near the top, there is a white cloud or mist through which the sun shines. It is very peaceful, and the climber is drawn through it towards the light of the sun. (This white cloud symbolises the cloud of unknowing, which we must penetrate in order to see with spiritual rather than physical eyes.) He is now attuned to a higher level of consciousness. This is rather a preparation for meditation than meditation itself. At the top of the mountain the mind feels empty, the body calm, and the meditation can begin. We can also use this mountaintop to meet and greet a teacher, enter a building, or simply ask for clarity about this or past lives.

A similar exercise is to raise awareness from the physical to the spiritual by contemplating each chakra from base to crown. Remember that the chakras are seven vital centres that go from the top of the head to the base of the spine. They are like power points, where lines of energy meet and cross. The chakras control the organs and glands of the body, and each one relates to a different frequency on the colour scale. The main chakras are:

1) The root, at the base of the spine. The related colour is red, and the gland is the gonads.
2) The spleen or sacral chakra, two or three inches below the navel. The related colour is orange, and the gland is the adrenals.
3) The solar plexus, at the diaphragm. The related colour is yellow, and the gland is the pancreas.
4) The heart, mid chest. The related colour is green, the gland the thymus.
5) The throat. The related colour is blue. The gland is the thyroid.
6) The brow, or third eye, in the centre of the forehead. The related colour is indigo, the gland the pituitary.
7) The crown chakra, at the top of the head. The related

colour is violet, the gland the pineal.

There is another centre, whose colour is white, about 18 inches above the crown, and others, including in the knees and feet, but it is more normal to focus on the seven I have just described.

Whether mountain or chakra meditation is used, remember to come down afterwards.

The flow of energy between the chakras affects our physical health as well as our sense of well-being, so it is a good idea to take care of them. (For details, see *Awakening to Change* and *The Power of Gems and Crystals.)*

Twenty years ago a technique to trigger past-life recall known as the 'Christos Experience' was very popular. The patient lies on the floor while one helper massages his forehead and another his feet. After a while the patient is instructed to imagine getting bigger and then smaller (a number of times), then to imagine floating out of his body and into the street until he feels able to soar above local buildings. He is then guided to return to earth in a different time and place and to describe what he sees. (I have never tried the Christos Experience myself, but understand it can be very successful. For those who want to try it it is imperative to buy A M Glaskin's book on the subject, which contains detailed instructions.)

Many past-life therapists guide their patients into and through a mist until they emerge on the other side in the memory of another life. There are many ways. What is important is to let the imagination play, and allow whatever images appear to surface without censorship.

Anxiety for immediate and/or dramatic results can interfere with the process. Sometimes it can take several sessions to gain clarity. Most of us *built* the pyramids rather than wafted around inside them as pharaohs, priests and priestesses.

Present And Pre-natal Regression

Present and pre-natal regression is just as important as regression into other lives. In fact, both can make journeys into the past much easier. I always include both in my own sessions. Present-life regression is a review of each year of this life from one's present age right back to childhood and birth. Pre-natal regression goes from birth to and through the nine months in the womb to conception and pre-conception. The latter is usually easier to do with a therapist.

The journey back to birth can be done as one big, long, meditative reverie, or in stages. For example, we can let our minds drift from what happened this week . . . to last month . . . to two years ago . . . five . . . ten years ago, and so on, until we arrive at our moment of birth. Or we can use one session thoroughly to cover a five or ten-year phase of life. In either case, we should review the best and worst events: illness and what it teaches us; chronic likes and dislikes; relationships with family, friends and others; habits we find hard to break; and mistakes (if we review these while we can still do something about them, we shall not carry them into our next incarnation. Remember that from the soul point of view there are no mistakes, only opportunities to learn.) We ought also to look at our emotions from the most negative to the most positive (do we express or stifle them?) Our happiest and saddest memories, attitudes to sexuality, pleasure, authority, work, money, food . . . and so on. The list is endless and we ourselves must decide on the other subjects and areas we need to examine.

During this process, stop at any scene that still holds the emotion of a particular event or problem. Do not be afraid to 'go into' or explore the feeling thoroughly – this discharges what has become 'stuck energy'. To re-live it releases it. Seth once said: 'Feelings are like the weather, don't be afraid of them. Feeling is the power out of which all realities emerge.' Our feelings, or even lack of them, can also be a bridge into past-life memory.

When we reach memories of childhood, especially the first seven years which are the most formative, we should thoroughly question our relationship with our parents: 'was my mother really there for me? . . . My father? . . .' We accept or reject our own femininity and masculinity from these role models, and need to see where the balance or imbalance originated.

(Another way of getting in touch with past-life memory is, either literally or imaginatively, to look into the eyes of parents, grandparents – and anyone else for that matter, including staring into our own eyes with the aid of a mirror – and mentally repeat: 'Where did I know you before?' After a few minutes the person's face will change, or images of other lives will float into the mind's eye.)

As children, we often adapt to the needs of others, and suppress our natural instinct to be ourselves. Many of these expectations come, not only from family, but also from school and society. If we can discover the source of any blocks and inhibitions, we can overcome them.

It is never too late to have a happy childhood. We can release any possible pressure to conform by using our imagination to recreate what really happened. (Remember that we are the directors of our own films. If they do not appear to be box-office successes, we can change the scenes in exactly the same way that a film director alters or re-creates his.)

The journey through birth, the womb, conception and

pre-conception is easier if it follows a similar process of, initially, drifting through the years of this life – but quickly, as if they were a dream – and without focus on any year or event. Then re-live the moment of birth. 'How did it feel? . . . Was it light? . . . dark? . . . cold? . . . warm? . . . frightening? . . . funny? . . .' Imagine being held by your mother . . . then your father, for the first time. 'How did that feel?' Then move back into the womb and go through each month. 'What was it like? Were there different colours? . . . sensations? . . . realisations? . . . or images for each month? or not?' Then imagine the moment of conception – was it happy, sad, easy, difficult? . . . and so on. Imagine the future parents' attitude to each other at this time, and why the soul chose them for this particular incarnation. From here it is relatively easy to go further back into the memories of pre-conception and in-between life.

A six-year-old child, when asked to describe his conception, drew lots of little circular-shaped blobs attached to balloons that floated from the sky to earth, until they converged in a mass around the roof of a house, which he said was his. When questioned further, the little boy said: 'They all want to come in, but there's no room. My friend came first to look out for me and keep a space for me in case I lost my way.' The child turned out to be a second-born twin.

Successful Recall

If we keep a journal or diary to record our dreams, past-life recall becomes much easier. In dreams, to see ourselves on a stage, to see geometric shapes, or even empty shelves, symbolises contact with the Akashic records. If we decide to use dreams as a method of Akashic contact, we should

191

remember to 'leave the day behind' before sleep. We can either sum up what the day has been by writing about it, or we can breathe the memory of it into a candle or crystal. We can also simply let the memory drain away by placing our feet in a bowl of warm water and consciously releasing it. We should then think of the question we want answered and write down: 'I want to dream. I want to remember my dream' followed by the question. (For further information on dreams, please see *Power of Your Dreams*.)

Successful past-life therapy is neither difficult nor peculiar. In fact, we reincarnate every day when we awake from the 'little death' of sleep. Regression or past-life therapy requires from those who choose to explore it openness, curiosity, patience, perseverance, humour and commonsense. It is not an escape from life but a process that we can use to live with greater effectiveness and creativity.

Many years ago Buddha wrote the following four 'Reliances':

> *Rely on the message of the teacher, not his*
>   *personality.*
> *Rely on the meaning, not just the words.*
> *Rely on the real meaning, not just the provisional*
>   *one.*
> *Rely on your wisdom mind, not on your ordinary*
>   *judgemental one.*

Past-life therapy is a path to this wisdom.

RECOMMENDED READING

Richard Bach, *Bridge Across Forever* (1994, Pan Books)

Richard Bach, *Illusions: Adventures of a Reluctant Messiah* (1994, Mandarin)

Richard Bach, *Jonathan Livingstone Seagull: A Story* (1994, HarperCollins)

Dannion Brinkley with Paul Perry, *Saved by the Light: The True Story of a Man Who Died Twice and the Profound Revelations He Received* (1993, Piatkus Books)

Ken Carey, *Return of the Bird Tribes* (1992, Harper SanFrancisco)

Sylvia Cranston and Carey Williams, *Reincarnation: A New Horizon in Science and Religion and Society* (1994, Theosophical)

Joseph Head and Sylvia Cranston, *Reincarnation: An East–West Anthology* (1989, Theosophical)

Elizabeth Kübler-Ross, *On Life After Death* (1993, Celestial Arts)

Denise Linn, *Past Lives, Present Dreams* (1994, Piatkus Books)

Barbara Marciniak, *Bringers of the Dawn: Teaching from the Pleiadians* (1993, Bear & Co)

Robert Monroe, *Journeys Out of the Body* (1989, Souvenir Press)

Dr Raymond Moody, *Life After Life* (1994, Bantam Books)

Dr Raymond Moody and Paul Perry, *Light Beyond* (1994, Macmillan)

Dr Melvin Morse with Paul Perry, *Closer to the Light* (1994, Bantam Books)

Dr Melvin Morse with Paul Perry, *Parting Visons: An Exploration of Predeath Psychic and Spiritual Experiences* (1995, Piatkus Books)

Dr Melvin Morse, *Transformed by the Light* (1993, Piatkus Books)

John J. O'Neill, *Prodigal Genius: Life of Nikola Tesla* (1994, Angriff Publishing)

James Redfield, *Celestine Prophecies* (1994, Bantam Books)

Sogyal Rinpoche, *The Tibetan Book of Living and Dying* (1994, Rider)

Jane Roberts, *How to Develop Your ESP Power: First Published Encounter with Seth* (1994, Lifetime Books)

Jane Roberts, *Nature of Personal Reality: Seth Book – Specific, Practical Techniques for Solving Everyday Problems and Enriching the Life You Know* (1994, New World Library)

Jane Roberts, *Seth Speaks: The External Validity of the Soul* (1994, New World Library)

Zecharia Sitchin, *Genesis Revisited: Is Modern Science Catching Up with Ancient Knowledge?* (1991, Bear & Co)

Dr Brian L. Weiss, *Many Lives, Many Masters: The True Story of a Prominent Psychiatrist, His Young Patient and the Past-life Therapy that Changed Both of Their Lives* (1994, Piatkus Books)

USEFUL ADDRESSES

Soozi Holbeche Workshops
c/o Maggie Roberts, 260 Kew Road, Richmond, Surrey
TW9 3EG, UK
Tel: 0181–948 4156

UK

Alexander Technique UK – SCAT
20 London House, 266 Fulham Road, London
SW10 9EL
Tel: 0171–352 0666

Aura Soma UK
Little London, Tetford, Lincs LN96 6OL
Tel: 01507 533441

Paul Solomon Tapes (and Soozi Holbeche Tapes)
c/o Inner Light Consciousness, PO Box 23, Yately,
Camberley, Surrey GU17 7FT

Australia

Australian Society of Teachers of the Alexander
Technique
83 Bronte Road, Bondi Junction, NSW 2022
Tel: 02 387 6999

Alexander Technique Ackers Training Centre
11 Stanley Street, Darlinghurst, NSW 2010
Tel: 02 331 7563

Alexander Technique Associates Teaching Centre
88a Hampden Road, Artarmon, NSW 2064
Tel: 02 411 7488

Alexander Technique Australia
Andrew Beesley, 245 Broadway, Sydney, NSW 2007
Tel: 02 552 2124

Academy Applied Hypnosis
Level 4, 300 George Street, Sydney, NSW 2000
Tel: 02 231 4877

Australian Hypnotherapists Association
20 Larool Crescent, Castle Hill, NSW 2154
Tel: 02 634 4915

Aura Soma Australia
Margaret and Harry Simon, 10 Signet Place, Llawong,
NSW 2234
Tel: 02 541 1066

Brucon Soma Centre
171 Victoria Road, Drummoyne, NSW 2047
Tel: 02 719 8143

Fabliss Health and Wellbeing Centre
Suite 225, 161 Military Road, Neutral Bay, NSW 2089
Tel: 02 953 8503

Past Lives Information Centre
10 Grose Street, Parramatta, NSW 2150
Tel: 02 683 4100

New Zealand

Aura Soma New Zealand
Diana Kirchin, 204 Plateau Road, Te Marna, Upper Hutt
Tel: 452 69718

South Africa

Alexander Technique South Africa
Yvonne Becker, 52 Main Road, Newlands 7700,
Capetown
Tel: 21 612 156

Aura Soma South Africa
Melissie Jolly, St Mary's Road, Kloof 3610, Durban
Tel: 31 764 5455

Creative Processes PTY Ltd
PO Box 726, Durbanville 7550
Tel: 21 975 2602
Fax: 21 975 2603

USA

The Monroe Institute (for the Monroe tapes)
Route Box 175, Faber, Virginia 22938

A.R.E. (Association for Research and Enlightenment)
PO Box 595, Virginia Beach, VA 23451

Kay Ortmans
Well-Springs, 21 N. Prospect Avenue, Madison,
Wisconsin 53705
Tel: 608 233 5188

INDEX

Index